The Problem of Evil

Key Concepts in Philosophy
Heather Battaly, *Virtue*
Lisa Bortolotti, *Irrationality*
Joseph Keim Campbell, *Free Will*
Roy T. Cook, *Paradoxes*
Douglas Edwards, *Properties*
Bryan Frances, *Disagreement*
Douglas Kutach, *Causation*
Ian Evans and Nicolas D. Smith, *Knowledge*
Joshua Weisberg, *Consciousness*
Chase Wrenn, *Truth*

The Problem of Evil

Daniel Speak

polity

The right of Daniel Speak to be identified as Author of this Work has been asserted in accordance with the UK Copyright, Designs and Patents Act 1988.

First published in 2015 by Polity Press

Polity Press
65 Bridge Street
Cambridge CB2 1UR, UK

Polity Press
350 Main Street
Malden, MA 02148, USA

ISBN-13: 978-0-7456-6406-4
ISBN-13: 978-0-7456-6407-1(pb)

A catalogue record for this book is available from the British Library.

Typeset in 10.5 on 12 pt Sabon
by Toppan Best-set Premedia Limited

The publisher has used its best endeavours to ensure that the URLs for external websites referred to in this book are correct and active at the time of going to press. However, the publisher has no responsibility for the websites and can make no guarantee that a site will remain live or that the content is or will remain appropriate.

Every effort has been made to trace all copyright holders, but if any have been inadvertently overlooked the publisher will be pleased to include any necessary credits in any subsequent reprint or edition.

For further information on Polity, visit our website: politybooks.com

Contents

Acknowledgments   vii

1   The Problem(s) of Evil   1
2   The Logical Problem   19
3   The Evidential Problem   47
4   The Problem of Divine Hiddenness   73
5   The Project of Theodicy   94
6   Tentative Conclusions and Beyond   115

Notes   129
Bibliography   140
Index   146

*For my wife, Lori Speak, whose love and friendship
remind me that evil will not have the last word*

Acknowledgments

Many thanks to Emma Hutchinson of Polity Press for her initial vision, wise counsel, and constant encouragement at each stage of this project. This book owes a great deal to the many students, both undergraduate and graduate, who have taken courses with me on the topic of the problem of evil over the past few years. I have learned particularly from Katherine Brown, Curtis Holtzen, Derek von Barandy, and Alex Zambrano. Two initially anonymous reviewers for Polity Press provided extremely useful feedback on a draft of the book. Raymond VanArragon in particular, who was kind enough to come out from behind his anonymity, made a substantial contribution to the overall quality of the manuscript and saved me from a number of embarrassments – including confusing the names of an influential human ecologist and a left-handed Houston Rockets shooting guard. Manuel Vargas read the entire manuscript and provided terrific suggestions throughout. A second special thanks to Katherine Brown for extraordinary copy editing and the construction of the index.

It was a great pleasure to serve as a Visiting Research Fellow at Biola University's *Center for Christian Thought* during the spring of 2013 and as a Visiting Scholar at Rutgers University's *Center for Philosophy of Religion* during the 2013/14 academic year. Both opportunities afforded me great freedom to work on this project while also providing me with nearly unlimited philosophical inspiration. Finally, I would like to thank Loyola Marymount University, the Bellarmine College of Liberal Arts, and the LMU Department of Philosophy for the sabbatical time that allowed me to take advantage of the various fellowship opportunities that made writing this book such a pleasure.

1

The Problem(s) of Evil

It is hard to know in advance what kind of suffering a person will have to see or experience before becoming gripped by the problem of evil. Bad-things-happening-to-children does, however, constitute a pretty reliable recipe for getting the attention of most people. I can report that my own sensitivities to the issues taken up in this book were profoundly heightened by having a child of my own and becoming, as a result, freshly attuned to the innocent vulnerability of children. I was already disposed to feel the burden of their seemingly senseless suffering (who isn't?), even before my son was born. But after his birth, my emotional nerves seemed to have been exposed painfully to the shocking air of moral reality. Reports of starving or abused children, of children forced to become slaves or soldiers, even popular movies featuring children under threat (pretend-children that I *knew* would be pretend-rescued near the end of the two-hour ordeal) all placed a new and swelling weight on my psyche.

I suspect that this is at least some part of the reason that the following experience still leaps immediately to mind when I find myself considering the world's evils. A decade or so back, when our son was still quite young, my wife and I were in the habit of getting together regularly (roughly, weekly) with a group of our friends at one of our homes. A little food, a little conversation, and the kids with a baby-sitter; a good evening for everyone, typically. The last time that group ever got together, however, was tragically memorable. I showed up at the home of the host, Mary, a smidge earlier than everyone else – to find a pair of police cars and Mary out front. Before I could get my car parked, it became clear that Mary was absolutely distraught. The explanation for her state turned out to be that her four-year-old son had drowned in their backyard pool some short time prior to my arrival. The son, Joshua, had evidently either climbed over the short protective pool fence by way of some bigger toys pressed up against it or had come through the gate accidentally left open by the pool cleaner, who had been by earlier in the day. In one sense, it doesn't really matter what the precipitating cause was. In either case, Joshua was dead and someone was going to be left feeling guilty for the rest of his or her life. In fact, maybe the best result was that we were never able to diagnose exactly how Joshua got into the pool area. Though both Mary and the pool cleaner will have to share the worry that each *may* have been the cause, neither of them has to bear the burden of certainly having been. Thank God for small mercies.

But, of course, that's just the point. It seems a pathetically small mercy in this context. After all, it is incredibly hard to shake the suspicion that it would have been very easy for a being with the qualities and powers typically ascribed to God to have kept Joshua from drowning. A light breeze to close the gate or the shifting of a plastic faux barbecue away from the fence is all it would have taken. If it is easier for God to put thoughts into heads than to move things around in the macro world, then a small and unobtrusive reminder for either the pool cleaner or Mary would easily have done the trick. For this reason, we can understand why Mary (or any of us who are able to sympathize with her pain and loss) might begin to wonder if God really does exist.

And now we are alive to the problem of evil – a problem constituted by an apparent tension between traditional theistic commitment, on the one hand, and an open-eyed recognition of countless instances of seemingly unjustified suffering, on the other. The family of philosophical challenges to theistic belief that we will be exploring can, in fact, be read as variations on a theme introduced in what David Hume called "Epicurus' old questions":

> Is [God] willing to prevent evil, but not able? Then he is
> impotent. Is he able, but not willing? Then he is malevolent.
> Is he both able and willing? Whence then is evil? (1947,
> 196)

Obviously, this problem has a long history. Thoughtful
people hoping to make sense of religious belief have almost
universally run upon it in one form or another. Epicurus was
raising this issue all the way back in the fourth century BCE
St. Augustine famously committed a great deal of his philosophical energy to it some fifteen hundred years ago. And in
the centuries since Augustine nearly every important thinker
has made some effort to address it. The problem of evil would
seem to have a fair claim, then, on being one of the most
perennial in philosophy. To be clear, however, this book is
not a *historical* introduction to the problem of evil. I will not
be making any particular effort to trace out the history of the
problem or explicate any of the important positions on it
developed prior to the twentieth century. Instead, my aim will
be to draw the reader into the incredibly lively contemporary
debate about the problem with an eye toward getting the
reader "up to speed" on the main and immediately pressing
issues.

I should add that I do not pretend to be indifferent to or
neutral with respect to the outcome of this debate. This introduction to the contemporary problem of evil is, rather, mildly
opinionated, and this is reflected both in the content I choose
to emphasize and in the substantive conclusions that I urge
the reader (again, mildly) to draw. Here let me remove any
obscurity regarding the conclusions I favor. In short, I will be
arguing that, the force of the various versions of the problem
of evil notwithstanding, *theistic commitment can nevertheless
be rational*. Notice that this is not to say that all theistic commitment is in fact rational or that it would be irrational to
draw agnostic or atheistic conclusions from the data of evil,
such as it is. The claim I will be defending, then, is actually
quite weak, even if it does amount to a gentle vindication of
theism (on the assumption that I succeed in defending it
adequately). Still, I think it is both more honest to approach
the problem in this way and more likely to bear dialectical
fruit – more likely, that is, to put you, the reader, in a position

to appreciate the nature and structure of the ongoing debates. In any case, with my intentions made clear, I trust you will now be able to subject my arguments and conclusions to the proper scrutiny without having to do the extra armchair psychologizing about my hidden agendas. I hope that it helps to see my philosophical and religious colors unambiguously unfurled.

1.1   The Structure of the Problem

Very generally, we have noted that our problem results from an apparent tension between two commitments – theistic commitment on the one hand, and a fairly commonsensical commitment to the existence of considerable evil in the world on the other. We should now be more specific about this tension.

The problem of evil is a problem for *theism*. That is, it is a problem for any view that is premised on the existence of a maximally powerful and maximally good creator and sustainer of the universe. There are, obviously, many versions of theism: Christian theism, Islamic theism, Jewish theism, etc. It is a sociological fact (interesting or not, I don't know) that contemporary philosophy of religion has been driven overwhelmingly by Christian thought. We will treat this emphasis on *Christian* theism, however, as an inessential accident. The problem is, after all, a general philosophical one facing all forms of theism.

For this reason, we will frame the problem explicitly in terms of what we can call "common theism" – in terms of those commitments shared by (held in common among) the world's principal theistic religions.[1] What are these? They aren't surprising, and I have hinted at them already. The common theist is committed to the following claims:

(1) God exists.
(2) God is omnipotent (there are no coherent limits to divine power).
(3) God is omniscient (there are no coherent limits to divine knowledge).

(4) God is omnibenevolent (there are no coherent limits to divine goodness).

(Keep in mind, in addition, that on my view the term "God" here is best understood as an honorific title applied properly only to the being who created the universe – and who sustains it, if such sustenance is necessary. The term is, then, more like "Queen" and less like "Elizabeth." Thus, "God" is not so much a proper name as the term for a position of honor that any being, with whatever name, who met the conditions would deserve.[2])

Notice, now, that the common theist accepts more than the mere existence of God. The common theist also insists that God is unlimited in power, knowledge, and goodness. These further commitments are crucial because it is largely in virtue of them that the problem of evil emerges. World-views according to which there is some creator of the universe but which make no commitment to this being's maximal greatness simply do not have to face the problem in its stark and standard form, for reasons that we will see shortly.

In addition to the four propositions above, we will also insist that the common theist accepts

(5) Evil exists.

It isn't perfectly clear just what "evil" is supposed to be in this context, and our ordinary talk about evil will not be of very much help. Frequently, our everyday language of evil is aimed at picking out something that is especially bad. We might say: "It is bad enough that he lied to his wife, but he also cheated on her with her best friend! That was downright *evil*." Or: "Yes, she has made some moral mistakes, but she isn't *evil*." With respect to our problem, however, the word "evil" doesn't apply only to particularly heinous or intensely morally disturbing events. The problem of evil, as we will be thinking of it, could also be called the problem of bad things, since it is the occurrence of anything less than good – from petty theft and the common cold all the way up to, and including, strategic genocide and the Lisbon earthquake – that generates it. The idea here is just that proposition (5) is asserting something quite bland and obvious to most folks:

namely, that bad things happen in our world. It may turn out that the occurrence of some especially gruesome evils makes the problem we are facing particularly difficult to handle. But we can set this aside for now. The problem itself is not about only these most gruesome evils but about bad things in general.

With propositions (1)–(5) out in the open, we can now sharpen the blade of the problem of evil for common theism. The problem is that these propositions appear to be in philosophical tension with one another. That is, there are reasons to think that these propositions either cannot or are not likely to be true together. The principal way that philosophers have brought out these reasons has been by formulating *arguments for atheism* based on the propositions endorsed by the common theist. The general strategy has been, in short, to try to show that anyone who accepts propositions (2)–(5) ought to reject proposition (1). The most influential of the specific versions of these arguments from evil for atheism will be the respective topics of the next three chapters. But it will help us here just to sketch them somewhat casually.

In chapter 2, we will take up what has typically been called the "Logical" or "Deductive" argument from evil. According to this argument, propositions (1)–(5) are *logically inconsistent*. It is logically impossible for all of them to be true together. Thus, anyone who accepts (2)–(5) is rationally required (on pain of contradiction) to give up (1). In chapter 3, we will turn to the "Evidential" or "Inductive" argument from evil. Here the claim will be *not* that (1)–(5) cannot possibly be true together, but that it is *unlikely* that they are. According to this argument, then, one who accepts (2)–(5) should give up (1), not because it is impossible for (1) to be true, but rather because it is improbable. Chapter 4 will address what has come to be known as the argument from "Divine Hiddenness." This argument appeals to a particular kind of evil we seem to find in abundance in the world: namely, reasonable unbelief in the existence of God. The idea here is that a good God would make sure that human beings were able to be in relationship to God. But many people seem not to be able to be in relationship to God because they are not able (try as they might) to believe that such a being exists. According to this argument, then, anyone who accepts (2)–(5)

and the claim that there are reasonable people who cannot believe in God should conclude that (1) is false.

To sum up, then, the problem of evil, as we will construe it, is a family of *prima facie* forceful arguments for atheism premised on a philosophical tension among the five propositions characterizing common theism.

1.2   The Structure of Response

Since the contemporary problem of evil is framed in terms of particular arguments for atheism, theistic replies will have to address these arguments. Depending on who you believe bears the various burdens of proof, however, there is more than one way to address an argument you take to lead to a false conclusion. Thinking about these possible burdens of proof and the potential kinds of replies available to theists will allow us to appreciate some subtleties in the structure of response to the problem of evil.

Suppose, for example, that you have been accused of a serious crime – armed robbery, say. The prosecuting attorney brings a case against you, the conclusion of which is that you are guilty of having entered a particular store on a certain date and of using a gun to force its owner to give you the money in the cash register. What the prosecutor purports to show, we might say, is that there is a deep tension in the set of propositions describing the actual circumstances at the time of the crime that also include the proposition that you did not commit the crime. If the prosecutor were a poor rhetorician with an unfortunate and slavish commitment to philosophical jargon, he might put his point by saying that the common propositions (those accepted even by *you* as the defendant) make it either impossible or extremely unlikely (so unlikely as to be beyond a *reasonable* doubt) that you are innocent. Now, in a U.S. court of law the prosecution must prove its case to establish your guilt, since you are stipulated to be innocent until proven guilty. This means that your innocence can be established simply by demonstrating that the prosecution has not made its case. All you have to do is show that the argument from what everyone accepts to your guilt *can reasonably be thought to fail.*

You can imagine, however, wanting something more than bare innocence under the law. For various reasons that have to do with your interests beyond your legal standing, you might be unsatisfied with having shown only that the prosecution didn't succeed in establishing your guilt. You might want, after all, *positive vindication* – you might, that is, hope to demonstrate to all and sundry that you did not in fact rob the store. What would it take to do this? It isn't easy to say, exactly. At the very least, though, you would have to show (to everyone who matters to you) not only that the appearance of your guilt was only an appearance but also *how* you are innocent – why it is quite reasonable to believe in your innocence despite the appearances.

So, these are two different ways to respond to an argument for the claim that you robbed the store, and they parallel the two different ways that theists can respond to an argument from evil for atheism. The theist can respond by attempting to show that the atheologian (the proponent of an argument for atheism) has not made her case and, therefore, that theistic commitment is "innocent" – not guilty of irrationality. If the theist responds in this way, then he is offering what has come to be called a *DEFENSE*. However, like you in your armed robbery case, the theist may want more in response to the problem of evil. The theist may not be satisfied with the Scotch verdict of "not proven" for atheism and, again for various reasons, might want to go on to provide a positive vindication of theism in the face of evil. If the theist attempts a positive vindication, then he is offering what has come to be called a *THEODICY*.

Somewhat more carefully, then, we can characterize these two types of responses to arguments from evil for atheism in the following ways.

- **A Defense**: shows *that* a particular argument from evil can reasonably be thought to fail (i.e., that the argument has not made it unreasonable to believe that the propositions of the theistic set obtain together). Thus, it shows that God may have morally sufficient reasons for permitting the evils to which the argument appeals.
- **A Theodicy**: shows *how* the theist can accommodate the evils to which a particular argument appeals (i.e., how the

propositions of the theistic set can reasonably be thought to obtain together). Thus, it shows what God's morally sufficient reasons for permitting the evils to which the argument appeals might very well be – that is, what they can reasonably be thought to be.

1.3   A Very Brief Précis

It could probably go without saying that, in general, defense is considerably less demanding than theodicy. Parrying a particular argument from evil is clearly easier than constructing a positive justification for God's permission of all the evils we find in the world. It is also worth noting that the lion's share of my response to the various problems of evil (especially in the next three chapters) will be offered in the spirit of defense rather than of theodicy. In chapter 2, for example, I will explore and defend the "free will defense" (especially as it has been developed by Alvin Plantinga) in response to the Logical Problem of Evil.

The defense I will muster, in chapter 3, in response to the Evidential Problem of Evil will have a number of independent (but potentially mutually supporting) prongs, chief among which is a prominent skeptical maneuver. The skeptical theist (who deploys this skeptical maneuver) is not skeptical about theism but instead about the value judgments that animate the Evidential Problem of Evil. Thus, according to skeptical theism we are (and should have expected ourselves to be) largely in the dark about what goods God is promoting and what evils God is avoiding by allowing a particular bad thing to occur. If this is right, then it is very difficult for the Evidential Problem to get off the ground.

In chapter 4 I turn to the Problem of Divine Hiddenness. As I mentioned above, the main issue here is that the existence of reasonable people who appear to be incapable of believing that God exists constitutes a very distinctive kind of evil that counts evidentially against the existence of that God. Here my defense will build on the defensive maneuvers of chapter 3, but also add a further consideration about the possibility of relationship with God without belief that God exists.

One natural question to ask, however, is whether defense is enough. In chapter 5, then, we will address the project of theodicy directly, asking in particular (and among other things) if the theist can rest content without one – provided, of course, that she has a compelling defense. I will be arguing (perhaps unsurprisingly) that as desirable as a theodicy might be under some conditions, a forceful defense is nevertheless enough to protect the basic rationality of theistic belief.

Finally, in chapter 6, I will bring these considerations together to offer my final (but nevertheless quite tentative) conclusions about the basic rationality of theistic belief. In a last effort to support these conclusions, I will be arguing that the atheist has a problem of her own in taking evil seriously – she has what I will call the "Problem of Profound Evil." In addition, we will return to reflect on the limitations of merely "common theism" in addressing the problems of evil. Perhaps we have been overly constrained by our commitment to abstracting away from particular religious traditions. Perhaps, that is, there are special resources within these particular religious traditions for dealing with the problem of evil. Again, the overarching conclusion I will be attempting to draw is not that the atheistic arguments from evil are without force or that the theist (either common or particular) has a demonstrably decisive reply to them. Instead, I hope to show only that even in the face of the quite challenging atheistic arguments from evil that have been developed in the contemporary debate, it can still be rational to maintain theistic commitment. More to the point of our purposes here, I aim to leave you in position to enter directly into this lively and important contemporary debate with a fuller understanding of its structure and content.

1.4   The Two Pulls of Evil

Before turning to the details in the next chapters, let me draw your attention to a frequently overlooked fact about the human experience with evil. This fact, as I am tendentiously calling it, is that our encounters with evil do not appear to pull us uniformly in the direction of unbelief. It is true, of course, that a great many people have been drawn to unbelief as a result of reflection on, or experience with, suffering and evil. At the same time, however, we should not ignore the fact that a great many people have also been drawn to theistic belief and religious commitment by such experiences. So-called "foxhole conversions" are one common instance of the pull *toward* religious commitment provoked by encounters with evil, but the phenomenon is quite widespread. In the face of suffering or danger or despair, many human beings find themselves reaching out to the transcendent – sometimes for help, sometimes for comfort, perhaps most deeply for explanation. And as it turns out, no small number of these people seem to discover enough of what they are looking for. The point here is that evil appears to have the power to pull us in two different directions. On the one hand, our confrontations with evil quite naturally provoke our suspicion that a maximally powerful and loving being could not permit it; down this path lies doubt and unbelief. On the other hand, these confrontations with evil can also cause us to see our profound limitations, deep ignorance, and shocking vulnerability. Seeing our own radical contingency provokes, again quite naturally, a longing to be grounded in a necessity beyond ourselves, with the full force of its buck-stopping explanatory power; down this path lies belief and commitment.

We could cull examples of the dual pull of evil from countless episodes in literary and cultural history.[3] But we can see an especially illuminating comparison and contrast of both coming from the single fertile mind of Fyodor Dostoevsky – who was quite personally gripped by the problem of evil.

In fact, his literary presentation of the problem, from the mouth of Ivan Karamazov, has a claim on being the most forceful ever narrated. In chapter 4 of *The Brothers Karamazov*, the older brother Ivan, worldly and sophisticated, confronts the younger Alyosha, a novice monk, with the harsh realities of nineteenth-century evil. Ivan describes a series of truly horrible "current events" involving (surprise!) the grave mistreatment of children. The final story is of an eight-year-old boy who is hunted for sport and killed by dogs in front of his mother at the command of an irritated land owner. Then, after a penetrating consideration of various justifications for these sorts of evils that a religious person might be tempted to offer, Ivan concludes:

> And if the suffering of children goes to make up the sum of suffering needed to buy truth, then I assert beforehand that the whole truth is not worth such a price. I do not, finally, want the mother to embrace the tormentor who let his dogs tear her son to pieces! She dare not forgive him! Let her forgive him for herself, if she wants to, let her forgive the tormentor her immeasurable maternal suffering; but she has no right to forgive the suffering of her child who was torn to pieces, she dare not forgive the tormentor, even if the child himself were to forgive him! And if that is so, if they dare not forgive, then where is the harmony? Is there in the whole world a being who could and would have the right to forgive? I don't want harmony, for love of mankind I don't want it. I want to remain with unrequited suffering. I'd rather remain with my unrequited suffering and unquenched indignation, *even if I am wrong*. Besides, they have put too high a price on harmony; we can't afford to pay so much for admission. And I hasten to return my ticket. (1982, 245)

Now, returning one's ticket needn't be the same thing as concluding that there is no maximally good being. In fact, Ivan explicitly claims not to be giving up on the existence of God, but instead to be lodging a kind of permanent protest against the divine plan. Still, many people have taken Ivan's claims to support and describe unbelief. At the very least, they give profound expression to the *pull* toward unbelief we can feel as we face evil.

By contrast, Dostoevsky's short story *The Dream of a Ridiculous Man*, published just prior to his writing *The Brothers Karamazov*, paints a different picture of the human response to evil. In the short story, the ridiculous man is being driven to suicide by his awareness of the meaninglessness of everything. His sense of this meaninglessness is so profound that, among other things, he finds himself completely unmoved by a child's desperate and sincere appeals for his help as he walks home to take his own life. On this night of his would-be suicide, he falls asleep with a pistol, his instrument of choice, in his hand – and has a life-changing "dream." He dreams that he is still awake and that he holds the pistol to his heart (though he had planned on shooting himself in the head) and pulls the trigger. He awakens from this "death" buried in a coffin. Eventually "some dark being" opens the grave and begins to carry the man through space. Amidst his fear and confusion, the man begins to realize that he is being taken to another earth, a kind of replica or double of our own. On this second earth, the man also finds that its inhabitants, human beings like us, are in what theologians might call a pre-fall state. They are joyful, loving, and simple. He lives among these beautiful and festive people, in various ways taking on their character and sharing in their fulfillment.

But the dream ends with the ridiculous man becoming the source of their corruption; he becomes the cause of their fall. He has brought with him from our earth a darkness in his soul that cannot be kept from them. And, as a result, he is forced to watch as the seed of his own sinfulness takes flower and yields its bitter fruit in the destruction of this humanity's innocence and happiness. Over the thousands of years that the man watches, the complete panoply of evil-doing takes its place on the scene: lying, grasping desire, jealousy, slavery, injustice of every conceivable kind. With the full picture of the suffering caused by evil before him, the ridiculous man comes to the end:

> Alas, I had always loved grief and sorrow, but only for myself, for myself, while over them I wept, pitying them. I stretched out my arms to them, in despair accusing, cursing, and despising myself. I told them that I, I alone, had done it all; that it was I who had brought them depravity, infection, and the lie! I beseeched them to crucify me on a cross, I taught them to make a cross. I couldn't, I hadn't the strength to kill myself, but I wanted to take the suffering from them, I longed for suffering, I longed to shed my blood to the last drop in this suffering. But they just laughed at me and in the end began to consider me some sort of holy fool. They vindicated me, they said they had received only what they themselves had wanted, and that everything could not but be as it was. Finally, they announced that I was becoming dangerous for them and that they would put me in a madhouse if I didn't keep quiet. Here sorrow entered my soul with such force that my heart was wrung, and I felt I was going to die, and here....well, here I woke up.

The man's response to his dream is particularly intriguing.

> Here suddenly, while I was standing and coming to my senses
> – suddenly my revolver flashed before me, ready, loaded –
> but I instantly pushed it away from me! Oh, life, life now! I
> lifted up my arms and called out to the eternal truth; did not
> call out but wept; rapture, boundless rapture, elevated my
> whole being. Yes life and – preaching! I decided on preaching
> that same moment and, of course, for the rest of my life! I'm
> going out to preach, I want to preach – what? The truth, for
> I saw it, saw it with my own eyes, saw all its glory.
> (316–17)

I hope it is obvious that this is a very different kind of response to the horrors of evil than the one Dostoevsky attributes to Ivan Karamazov. Ivan seems to see the evil as, in some fundamental sense, God's fault. And, as a result, he asks for his ticket back. The ridiculous man has come to see the evil as – and here the point is delicate – partly, or even largely, a matter of his own will; the problem is not with God but with himself, with the human heart. Thus, he is prepared not only to keep his ticket but also to get busy with the hopeful work of helping people to see what can be done to counteract or eliminate the suffering in the world.

To be clear, I haven't invoked these episodes from Dostoevsky in order to vindicate some particular position in the debate over the problem of evil. I don't think, for instance, that Dostoevsky's ridiculous man *answers* Ivan's challenge.[4] Insofar as Ivan has offered an argument, the ridiculous man has explicitly offered neither a theodicy nor a defense. The point of drawing our attention to these literary images, again, is to bring out the two different impulses of response to the realities of evil that we can find in ourselves. For all I have said here, one of these responses may, at the end of the day, be inherently more rational than the other or both may turn out to be incoherent or inapt. These narratives cannot settle the philosophical dispute. I do hope, though, that reflection on these cases and on the two different pulls of evil will allow us to contextualize the contemporary debate over the problem of evil more fairly and with greater sensitivity to what might be moving the interlocutors on both sides.

1.5   Warning Ourselves

Allow me to conclude this chapter with a warning – to you and me both. A few years back, I was teaching an introductory philosophy course to a small group of precocious honors students. They were smart, interesting, engaged, and prepared to get on board with the dialogical and exploratory methods of the discipline. We were using various issues in the philosophy of religion as our subject matter. We had already explored the "faith and reason" debate, the pros and cons of the traditional theistic arguments, and the possibilities for non-evidential justifications for religious belief when we turned to the problem of evil. The students were uniformly intrigued by the problem and began to work out the intellectual puzzle with burgeoning skill and vigor. When this class session ended, I was thoroughly pleased with the philosophy that had been done. They understood the central argument we had been focused upon, they had subjected it to serious and subtle scrutiny, and they were clearly developing their philosophical acumen; in fact, there wasn't much more that I (*qua* philosophy professor) could have hoped for from them during this class session.

Shortly after that class session ended, and while I was still basking in the glow of its intellectual success, there was a knock on my office door. It was one of the honors students from the class, an especially thoughtful and earnest young lady who had already set herself apart with respect to intelligence and sensitivity. She wanted to talk a bit further about this "problem of evil" we had introduced in class and that was going to be on the docket for the next few sessions. As I wound up my mind for some further abstract intellectual exercise, she stopped me short with her concrete encounter with evil. This young lady, striving sincerely to be a person of religious faith, described her father's ongoing battle with Amyotrophic Lateral Sclerosis (ALS, also known as Lou Gerhig's Disease). A vibrant person of faith himself and a wonderful husband and father, this once active man had now lost nearly all control of the muscles in his body. As the motor neurons in his brain and spine had degenerated, he had become increasingly a prisoner in his own frame, unable to use it to manipulate his environment, feed himself, or even express himself. By the time of our conversation, my student was the last person who could understand her father's slurred and labored speech; and, as a result, she spent a great deal of time as his translator to the rest of the family. She knew that she, too, would soon be unable to make anything of his efforts to communicate. He would soon be locked silently in the citadel of his own consciousness. She was, quite reasonably, terrified for her father on this score. To add to the tragedy both of her father's suffering and of her vicarious participation in it, she was also, she cautiously revealed, being forced to confront her own shameful responses. She found herself tired of the constant demands of her father's condition, even annoyed at him – and for what? For getting ALS? For being unable to eat on his own? For not being able to make himself understood? For casting a dark shadow over her own promising life? Obviously, she emphasized, she knew that all of this was selfish and confused. But there it was. Her father's life was devolving into a living hell and she was, at some level, feeling put out by it. Even thinking back about that conversation now, I am freshly moved by the deep and perverse pain of the whole situation.

My warning, then, is not to confuse the *philosophical* problems of evil (the admittedly real and potent intellectual challenges which are the focus of this book) with what we might call the *personal* problem of evil. The philosophical problems confront us with questions about how to think coherently about the relationship between God and evil. The personal problem, by contrast, is a matter of how to live with it: how to survive it and even counteract it, in our own lives and in the world more generally. There are various dangers that we face in running these two sets of issues together, not least of which is that no one facing one of them will be at all satisfied by responses that address the other.

What my sensitive student needed when she came to my office was not (or at least was not *only*) a more rigorous set of categories for thinking through the philosophical tensions among the claims endorsed by theists. What she needed, I presume, was empathy, support, and understanding. What we can offer the person who faces the personal problem of evil will have to be concrete and context-sensitive, because the problem is itself painfully concrete and contextual. It is *this very suffering* right here before us (whether our own or another's) that we face: no abstract concept of evil, no sterile historical instance. Thus, whatever help we can provide will have to be of the kind we can offer even without any especially compelling explanation of the existence of evil or of its compatibility with the fundamental goodness of God. In other words, philosophy isn't of much use here. Instead, the personal problem of evil can best be addressed by listening, by providing meals, by helping to carry the load, by telling our own story of living through pain, by invoking the stories of others, and (if you can talk yourself into it) by praying. Again, this is to say that it is generally a serious mistake to respond to the personal problem of evil with philosophy.[5]

Without distinguishing these two problems, then, we might fall into the trap of offering philosophical arguments when we should instead be offering a hug. Similarly, we might make the converse mistake of failing to reason carefully when careful reasoning is called for, perhaps because we have wrongly understood our interlocutor as in need of emotional rather than intellectual support. My own sense is that a great deal of the frustration with, and disparagement of, the contemporary project of theodicy is due to a general failure to appreciate the distinction here. As we will see in some detail in chapter 5, a number of recent thinkers have lodged moral complaints about the *very idea* of attempting to justify God's permission of the evils we find in the world. There is something morally untoward, so these theorists claim, simply in *trying* to develop a theodicy. Insofar as the problem of evil is a personal one, I can fully appreciate their point. Offering a theodicy to someone who is asking only how to make it through her evil-tarnished life will very likely make her suffering worse. If, as I suggest, however, the philosophical problems of evil are the ones being addressed, then it is far less clear that theodicy is morally inappropriate (again, this is a point I will develop in chapter 5).

A corollary to my warning is that the reader should not expect satisfying responses to the philosophical problems of evil to eliminate suffering or even make it easier to bear.[6] For some people, to be sure, the easing of philosophical tensions does also make the personal burden lighter. But there is no necessary connection here. And the practical point is this: we ought not evaluate the success of various responses to the philosophical problems of evil by the degree to which these responses help us deal better with concrete human suffering. Dealing with concrete human suffering is one thing. Dealing with the intellectual tensions that the existence of concrete human suffering creates is, in some respects, another.

I remain grateful for the conversation my student started with me that day after class. I was quite sincerely humbled by it, and the switch from philosopher to friend that it demanded of me has had a lasting impact. In fact, my recollection of the conversation continues to remind me not only of the distinction between the philosophical and personal problems of evil, but also of the fact that we do not do our philosophizing in a vacuum. Though I am recommending that we keep these two sets of problems distinct in our thinking, there is no question that they interpenetrate in each of us. Remember, then, that though I will be trying to argue that theistic belief can remain rational even in full view of the facts of evil, I will make every effort not to minimize these facts, tempting as it can sometimes be, from a rhetorical point of view, to do so. We owe all those who suffer at least this much.

2
The Logical Problem

Establishing the first moment of the "contemporary" in any domain inevitably involves a certain amount of arbitrariness. With this said, it isn't completely arbitrary to treat the publication, in 1955, of J. L. Mackie's essay "Evil and Omnipotence" as the initial salvo in the contemporary debate over the problem of evil.

Obviously, as I have already emphasized, evil has been taken to be a problem for theistic commitment from philosophical time immemorial. However, Mackie's argument introduced a distinctly argumentative structure into the debate. That is, Mackie formulated his complaint, as we will see, quite explicitly as an argument against the claim that God exists. By contrast, while the history of the discussion certainly brought evil to bear on the rationality of religious belief, this aspect of the problem was frequently enmeshed with a related but distinct problem of *explanation*. As a case in point, Leibniz, in his *Theodicy*, often treats the problem principally as having to do with how theism can account for the existence of evil rather than as a worry that God does not exist. The same, I think, can be said even for Hume's treatment of the issue in his *Dialogues Concerning Natural Religion*.[1] Prior to Mackie's challenging argument, the existence of evil was taken not so much as a consideration favoring atheism but more commonly as the source of an explanatory gap that theism should try either to fill or explain away.

Conceived of in this way, the problem is essentially internal to theism, and the failure of theism to address it satisfactorily might have been just one more place at which theologians and philosophers of religion were called upon to continue the ongoing work of rendering the theistic worldview acceptably coherent to its adherents. Like the doctrine of the Trinity or the package of issues regarding divine foreknowledge, the problem of evil might only have structured a theological project rather than a deep challenge to the existence of God. Mackie's argument and its profound influence decisively changed all of this – and made it impossible for philosophers of religion, in particular, to treat the existence of evil merely as an explanatory problem internal to the religious point of view. In doing this, Mackie's argument set the agenda for the philosophical discussion of the problem of evil that has ensued in the decades since.

2.1   Mackie's Argument

The initial grip and the enduring power of Mackie's argument are to be found in both its boldness and its clarity. With respect to its elegant boldness, Mackie positions his argument as a more forceful alternative to the traditional atheistic strategy of attack on the standard theistic arguments. The problem with the traditional strategy, he notes, is that the theist can, in principle, accept the full range of complaints about the various arguments for the existence of God without being rationally required to give up theistic belief. The argument he offers, however, can, he thinks, cut deeper than the traditional strategy.

Mackie begins thusly:

> The traditional arguments for the existence of God have been fairly thoroughly criticized by philosophers. But the theologian can, if he wishes, accept this criticism. He can admit that no rational proof of God's existence is possible. And he can still retain all that is essential to his position, by holding that God is known in some other, non-rational way. I think, however, that a more telling criticism can be made by way of the traditional problem of evil. Here it can be shown, not that

religious beliefs lack rational support, but that they are posi-
tively irrational, that the several parts of the essential theological doctrines are inconsistent with one another, so that the
theologian can maintain his position as a whole only by a
much more extreme rejection of reason than in the former
case. He must now be prepared to believe, not merely what
cannot be proved, but what can be *disproved* from other
beliefs that he also holds. (1955, 25)

The boldness here shouldn't be undersold. Mackie intends to
produce an argument that will render theistic belief "posi-
tively irrational" by revealing its essential inconsistency. If he
succeeds, then theistic belief will be worse than belief in the
existence of Bigfoot or the Loch Ness Monster: though the
existence of these controversial creatures is woefully unsupported by compelling evidence, at least there is no conceptual
incoherence built into the idea of either. Theistic belief will,
rather, be like belief in the existence of round squares or in
the existence of two things equal to a third thing that are not
equal to each other. We don't reject the existence of these
items on evidential grounds, but because to do otherwise is
to accept contradictions. On Mackie's reasoning, then, the
thesis that God exists doesn't so much as rise to the level of
being a proper object of evidential concern. The Chupacabra
should have it so bad.[2]

But boldness is not the only virtue of Mackie's argument.
The argument is also admirably clear. What Mackie emphasizes is that the problem of evil, as he is conceiving of it, is a
logical one (and thus the title customarily given to his argument).[3] It is a problem with the logical relations among the
things that the theist claims to believe.

In its simplest form the problem is this: God is omnipotent;
God is wholly good; and yet evil exists. There seems to be
some contradiction between these three propositions, so that
if any two of them were true the third would be false. But at
the same time all three are essential parts of most theological
positions: the theologian, it seems, at once *must* adhere and
cannot consistently adhere to all three. (1955, 25)

The effort to make this apparent contradiction evident is the
soul of the logical problem of evil and of Mackie's argument.

The intuitive idea would seem to follow upon the questions we earlier saw raised by Epicurus. If God exists and is omnipotent, then God is able to create a world without evil. If God exists and is wholly good, then God wants to create a world without evil. Thus, the fact of evil in the world is logically inconsistent with the existence of an omnipotent and wholly good God.[4]

Mackie recognizes, however, that this intuitive idea needs fleshing out. Specifically, he recognizes that the existence, omnipotence, and omnibenevolence of God do not strictly entail that there is no evil. In other words, Mackie has a little work to do to reveal that there is a formal contradiction in the set of propositions that the theist accepts. To do this work, Mackie proposes (or invokes) two additional propositions: one regarding goodness and one regarding power. The goodness proposition is that a good thing always eliminates evil as far as it can. The power proposition is that there are no limits to what an omnipotent thing can do. Taken together, now, Mackie believes that a contradiction is in the offing. One crisp way of seeing the supposed contradiction is by formulating Mackie's argument as a *reductio ad absurdum*. Thus, Mackie is convinced that the following five propositions

(1′) God exists.
(2′) God is omnipotent.
(3′) There are no limits to what an omnipotent being can do.
(4′) God is omnibenevolent.
(5′) A good being eliminates evil as far as it can.

together entail

(6′) Evil does not exist.

But (6′) is the *absurdum*; it is obviously false – and, indeed, the *theist herself* will insist that this is so. Since (6′) is false, claims (1′)–(5′) cannot all be true together (since they entail an obvious falsehood). That is, this set of claims must be logically inconsistent. Insofar as the theist accepts all six claims, she appears to be accepting a contradiction. This is surely the most damning complaint a philosopher can muster against a view.

After attempting to make explicit the logical inconsistency in the set of propositions the theist endorses, Mackie spends the lion's share of his famous article considering and criticizing anticipated responses to his argument, a number of which have been influential in the history of philosophical reflection on the problem of evil. In fact, we will have occasion to reflect somewhat more deeply and in particular upon Mackie's response to the invocation of human free will in response to his argument. For now, though, we should take note of the fact that Mackie appears to be aware that his extra premises – (3′) and (5′) – are controversial. He recognizes, particularly, that the theistic tradition has been willing to impose, at the very least, *logical* constraints on the power of an omnipotent being, *contra* (3′). Mackie is prepared to treat this concession (as he seems to be thinking of it) as something of an embarrassment to theism. He notes that, "a few have been prepared to deny God's omnipotence, and rather more have been prepared to keep the term 'omnipotence' but severely to restrict its meaning, recording quite a number of things that an omnipotent being cannot do" (1955, 26). There is a nice bit of rhetorical implicature here that the natural or common-sensical theistic view of omnipotence is being contorted into this untoward shape by the ad hoc effort to address Mackie's problem. But we should be clear that this isn't the case.[5] The framing of omnipotence in terms of the absence of logical constraints on power (which I adopted in the first chapter by suggesting that there are no *coherent* limits on what an omnipotent being can do) is certainly at the center of the theistic tradition, going back at least to Thomas Aquinas. Furthermore, the motivation for this position is essentially philosophical and largely independent of any particular problem facing theism.

More critically, and quite apart from its intellectual pedigree, we can see that the acceptance of this "constrained" view of omnipotence, far from being a tactic to avoid it, is actually a *precondition* for the logical problem that Mackie proposes. Without it, the problem he presses against theism simply evaporates. Why so? In short, because without it, the theist would have an easy reply to Mackie's objection. If there really are *no* limits on what an omnipotent being can do, logical or otherwise, then an omnipotent being can perform logical contradictions. That is, an omnipotent being can bring it about that contradictions are true. Thus, such a being can make a square every point of which is equidistant from a center point, can make 2 + 2 equal to 5, can make a three-sided figure the interior angles of which add up to 128, can make a door with only one side, can make an object that exists and does not exist at the same time and in the same way, and on it goes. The logical problem of evil, however, is supposed to reveal that theism involves a contradiction – and what is supposed to be so bad about this is that, of course, contradictions are necessarily false. But wait! If we accept the unconstrained conception of omnipotence, then God can perform logical contradictions; that is, God can bring it about that contradictions are *true*! So the theist who accepts this radical conception of omnipotence will be able to respond to the supposed contradiction exposed by Mackie's argument simply by appealing to God's power to bring it about that propositions (1′)–(6′) are all true together. Sure, this theist can grant, they involve a contradiction – so what? God is more powerful than logic. Without the logical "constraint" on the concept of omnipotence, then, Mackie's argument would be without force because any appeal to contradiction could be undercut by the divine power to render contradictions true.

Setting aside Mackie's rhetorical stretch on this point, however, the larger problem he formulates is quite powerful; and even beyond its philosophical power, the argument has been remarkably important. In part, this is because the philosophical work done in response to it has turned out to be both highly influential and of a very high caliber. Having said this, it is an interesting piece of philosophical sociology that one crucial response to Mackie's argument has widely been taken to be absolutely decisive. Let this sink in. What I am saying here is that many philosophers – unwilling, as they generally are, to take *any* arguments to be decisive, whether against Platonism about numbers or against Berkeley's idealism or against Leibniz's monadology or against Lewis's possible worlds – converge on the view that Mackie's argument has been decisively refuted. Furthermore, there is wide agreement that this refutation is due to a single response: namely,

Alvin Plantinga's Free Will Defense.[6] To illustrate, Robert Adams, speaking of the logical problem, has insisted that "it is fair to say that Plantinga has solved this problem. That is, he has argued convincingly for the consistency of [the set of propositions endorsed by the theist]" (1985, 226). Of course, neither the declaration of one prominent philosopher nor any amount of discipline-wide agreement with the declaration can establish it. For that, we need the arguments themselves and our own fair-minded assessments of them. Still, I think it would be reasonable for us, in light of the sentiments of the philosophical community, to turn to these arguments with especially lively attention.

2.2   The Free Will Defense

Plantinga's Free Will Defense involves a number of technicalities and subtleties, and we will have to sort out these details eventually. But the central strategy is quite simple and straightforward. To see it, let's remind ourselves of what a defense, in response to the logical argument from evil, aims to do. In general, a defense attempts to show that a particular atheistic argument from evil has not succeeded in establishing its conclusion. Since Mackie's logical problem purports to demonstrate that the set of common theistic propositions is logically inconsistent, a defense in response to this argument needs to show only that logical inconsistency has not been demonstrated – it needs to show only, that is, that all of the propositions that compose the commitments of common theism *could,* for all Mackie's argument says, still be true together. As a further reminder – and to have an easy way to refer to them – let's call the following set of commitments of common theism (introduced in chapter 1) the *Theistic Set:*

(1) God exists.
(2) God is omnipotent (there are no coherent limits to divine power).
(3) God is omniscient (there are no coherent limits to divine knowledge).

(4) God is omnibenevolent.
(5) Evil exists.

Notice, then, that a defense in response to Mackie's argument will not have to show that God exists or that God probably exists. Mackie is claiming that there is a fundamental logical contradiction embedded in the theistic set. To show the failure of his argument, it will be enough to show merely that it is *possible* for the theistic propositions all to be true at the same time. And, again, at the risk of being annoying, I emphasize that this is because Mackie (and the proponent of the logical problem more generally) is claiming that it is, in fact, *impossible* for all of them to be true together.

I have taken the risk of annoying you by harping on this last logical point because understanding it is crucial to appreciating the Free Will Defense – and I will add, for what it is worth, that popular treatments of Plantinga's defense frequently miss this point. In essence, then, it is the very argumentative boldness of Mackie's formulation of the problem that sets such a low bar for the success of a counterargument. If someone claims to identify a contradiction in my commitments, I have defended my commitments from this attack merely by showing that they *may* not be inconsistent.

In formulating his free will defense, then, Plantinga took his charge to be to show that it is possible for all five propositions of the theistic set to be true together. In other words, his aim was to show that there is a *possible world* (a way the world could have been) in which God exists; God is omnipotent, omniscient, and omnibenevolent; and evil exists. I find it illuminating to think of Plantinga's defense as unfolding in two stages.[7] At Stage I, Plantinga attempts to show that Mackie and other proponents of the logical problem of evil have not yet formalized the inconsistency that they purport to sense in the theistic set. This is the purely defensive stage of the defense. At Stage II, however, the defense goes on the offensive. At this stage Plantinga attempts to show that no effort to formalize the inconsistency can succeed. The big conclusion, then, is not only that no version of the logical problem of evil *has in fact* demonstrated that God does not exist (Stage I), but further that no future version *can ever* do so (Stage II).

2.3 Stage I

Plantinga's initial goal was to make it clear that no proponent of the logical problem of evil has quite completed the requisite task. That is, no one has so far been able to demonstrate that the theistic set is *formally* inconsistent. Now, what would it take to demonstrate this? Well, the logical-problematizer would need to present us with a set of propositions "contained" in the theistic set (either explicitly or implicitly) that entail a strict contradiction – which are such that it is impossible for all of them to be true together. Thinking back about Mackie's argument, it is clear that he saw the problem here to some degree. The fact that he recognized the need for his additional premises about goodness and power (which he also calls "quasi-logical rules") reveals his awareness of the fact that the supposed inconsistency in the theistic set is not completely transparent. At this first stage of his defense against the logical problem of evil, then, Plantinga sought to show that no compelling account of the formal inconsistency in the theistic set has yet been produced.

We need to get just a bit clearer on what Plantinga is demanding of his Mackie-style interlocutor. Since the logical problem is supposed to reveal an inconsistency in the things the theist endorses, the onus, at this stage, is on the proponent of the logical problem to show us what it is in the set of theistic commitments that entails a contradiction. Since propositions (1)–(5), constituting the theistic set, do not explicitly entail a contradiction, the contradiction will have to come from additional commitments *that the theist must accept* but that haven't been made explicit in the theistic set. What propositions *must* the theist accept? Presumably, just these: propositions that express necessary truths (*everyone* has to accept necessary truths!) and propositions expressing commitments that are essential to theism (surely the theist has to accept what is essential to theism).[8] So, now we have the challenge. If you want us to conclude that the theistic set is inconsistent, then produce a proposition we can reasonably suspect is either a necessary truth or essential to theism and which is such that, when added to the existing theistic set, it entails a contradiction. At the heart of this first stage of

Plantinga's reply to the logical problem is the claim that producing such a proposition is much more difficult than the proponents of the argument have been eager to admit.

For example, Plantinga notes that Mackie's own effort fails this demand. Recall that Mackie urges us to include

(5′) A good being eliminates evil as far as it can.

But this won't do. Far from being a necessary truth, it doesn't even appear to be a truth at all. We may grant that my throbbing headache is an evil. And a doctor could, of course, eliminate this headache by surgically removing my head. Doing so, however, would be no sign of this doctor's goodness. And why not? Because she would be destroying a greater good (let's suppose!) by employing this radical headache-relief strategy.[9] This means that Mackie's premise will need to be replaced with something more like

(5″) A good being eliminates evil as far as it can, provided that [it is reasonable for the being to believe that], in doing so, no greater goods are destroyed and no worse evils are created.[10]

Maybe the theist should accept (5″). But no contradiction will be immediately in the offing if the theist does so. To get the contradiction, the theist would also have to accept something like

(GG) An omnipotent and omnibenevolent being could have eliminated the evil we find in the world without destroying greater goods and without creating worse evils.

Is the theist under any compulsion to take on GG, however? Pretty clearly not. To insist that it is a necessary truth would be both highly presumptuous and question-begging in the extreme. And there is certainly no reason to think that it is a proposition essential to theism (far from it!). It looks, then, as if the formal inconsistency isn't going to be found in this direction.

The fuller version of Stage I involves running through various alternative possible propositions that might be thought to do the required work and, in each case, dismissing them on compelling grounds (1967, 118–30). But I won't reproduce Plantinga's detailed case here. Instead, I will simply highlight why I am inclined to think it succeeds in its goal (which, again, is to show both that no one has yet produced a proper version of the inconsistency proposition and that it is much harder to produce one than might initially have been supposed). In short, I am inclined to think that a proposition that can do the work required of it by Mackie's inconsistency goals will have either to be or entail

> (NR) There are no good reasons for an omnipotent, omniscient, and omnibenevolent being to permit evil.

Clearly, with NR in place, the proponent of the logical problem will be able to get a contradiction in the theistic set. But even if it is an open question whether or not NR is true (and I grant that it may be), it surely doesn't follow either that NR is a necessary truth or that it expresses a commitment essential to theism. In other words, the theist is within her epistemic rights, at this stage in the argument, to reject it. I submit that without something very much like NR, no formal contradiction is to be found. And yet, at the same time, NR is in no way forced upon the theist. The case here is not by any means decisive. I may be wrong that a contradiction in the theistic set can only be established by establishing something like NR. Or I may be wrong that the theist need not accept NR. Still, I take these claims to have enough initial plausibility to justify confidence in the success of Stage I of Plantinga's defense. We should conclude, with Plantinga, that the formal contradiction has not been established and that it is going to be very hard ever to establish it.

2.4 Stage II

We can turn now to the second, more aggressive and, in some respects, more interesting stage of Plantinga's defense. If the first stage was aimed at showing that inconsistency in the theistic set has not been demonstrated, this second stage attempts to go further by demonstrating that the theistic set is, in fact, *formally consistent*. That is, this portion of Plantinga's argument purports to demonstrate that no proposition of the form we were seeking above can even *possibly* be found.

His strategy at this stage can be seen as somewhat like the mirror image of the one he pressed upon those who hope to formalize the inconsistency in the theistic set. There, Plantinga urged his interlocutor to find a proposition the theist must accept that, taken together with the theistic set, entails a contradiction. Here, he hopes to turn the tables by finding a proposition consistent with propositions (1)–(4) of the theistic set that, together with them, entails (5): namely, that evil exists. If there is such a proposition (that merely *could* be true), then the theistic set cannot be inconsistent and Mackie's argument fails.

Plantinga purports to find such a proposition in a familiar story about human freedom and God's intentions. The story goes like this. It was very important for God to bring into existence creatures with free will. Such creatures (and only such creatures) would be capable of the fullest kinds of relationships both with God and with each other. Only with free will could there be the deepest goods of mutual love and moral responsibility. Thus, in order for God to create a world containing these deepest goods, it was necessary that human beings be endowed with the power to choose freely – even though this power would entail the possibility that human beings would go terribly wrong and use their freedom in self-destructive ways. If, in creating human beings thus, God has brought about a world in which there is considerable evil resulting from the free choices of these beings, there can be no complaint against God. The complaint must be leveled, rather, against those free beings who have used their freedom badly. This is because it is in the nature of freedom that it cannot be forced or guaranteed to be directed only at the good. If God had made human beings so that they could not possibly go wrong, then these beings would not have been free. The freedom of these creatures, then, was necessary for the possibility of great goods – goods so great as to justify God in bringing them into existence in spite of the logically necessary consequence of the risk of the evil. It will be true under these conditions that God has brought about the *possibility* of evil. But God has not brought about the evil itself. The evil itself rests with the human beings. The big and general point is that, according to the free will defender, it may have been *impossible* for God to create a world containing the goods we find without it also containing the evils.

What, then, is supposed to be the proposition consistent with (1)–(4) of the theistic set that, taken together with them, entails (5)? It isn't a tidy proposition, whatever it is. Here is one possible formulation of it:

> (C) Free will is necessary for the highest goods *and* it was impossible for God to create a world containing free will without also creating a world containing evil.

This proposition is *prima facie* consistent with God's existence, omnipotence, omniscience, and omnibenevolence. It also appears to entail that evil exists.[11] If this is true, then the logical problem of evil is dissolved. The theistic set is not formally inconsistent.

We have now seen the fundamental intuitive structure of Plantinga's free will defense. Its deeper ingenuity and intrigue emerge from Plantinga's extended response to a potentially powerful objection to the intuitive picture we have just painted.

2.5   Power and Possible Worlds

We said above that (C) was *prima facie* consistent with (1)–(4) of the theistic set. The important objection that Plantinga's defense had to face, however, is grounded in the suggestion that there is an *ultima facie* inconsistency. That is, after thinking more carefully about what (C) claims, it might reasonably be thought to be in logical conflict with the claim that God exemplifies all of the omnis. Even if we allow omnipotence to be "constrained" by logical coherence (as we should), there seems to be nothing blocking God from bringing about a world with free creatures who do not use their freedom badly. This is because *logic* doesn't demand that free will be used badly. Put another way, among all the ways the world could have been, one of these ways involves every free creature using his or her freedom to do only what is right and good. Since the only constraints on God's omnipotence are logical ones, and since there is nothing logically contradictory about a world wherein all the free creatures choose only what is right and good, God should have been able to bring this world into existence.

Here is Mackie, pressing this point:

> If God has made men such that in their free choices they sometimes prefer what is good and sometimes what is evil, why could he not have made men such that they always freely choose the good? If there is no logical impossibility in a man's freely choosing the good on one, or on several occasions, there cannot be a logical impossibility in his freely choosing the good on every occasion. God was not, then, faced with the choice between making innocent automata and making beings who, in acting freely, would sometimes go wrong; there was open to him the obviously better possibility of making beings who would act freely but always go right. Clearly, his failure to avail himself of this possibility is inconsistent with his being both omnipotent and wholly good. (1955, 33)[12]

The challenge, then, should be clear. For (C) to be consistent with propositions (1)–(4) of the theistic set, the impossibility of God's creating a world with free creatures who always choose rightly must not be due to some genuine limitation on God's power or goodness. To save the free will defense, the limitation would have to be a broadly logical one. But, according to Mackie, there is no logical incoherence in the concept of a world in which all free creatures always choose rightly. Thus, we should conclude that (C) is not consistent with (1)–(4), initial appearances notwithstanding. If this is right, then the free will defender has not shown that it is possible for the theistic set to be consistent. Understanding Plantinga's response to this challenge will require us to venture somewhat deeply into the metaphysics of modality (i.e., the metaphysics of possibility and necessity). My apologies in advance.

Let's start with a tempting thought, the one that appears to be underwriting Mackie's objection above. If the only limits on God's power are logical ones, then God can do anything that is not logically impossible. In particular, it is very tempting to think that God can create *any* complete world that involves no logical contradictions. Though Mackie never explicitly appeals to this thought, notice that he needs something like it. Without it, he cannot get from the fact that *a world with free beings who always choose rightly involves no logical contradiction* to the claim that *God could have (and therefore should have) made this one like that.* Given how tempting the thought is, it may come as a surprise that Plantinga argues quite potently against it.

To see how this argument goes, we will need some new concepts and technical terminology. Earlier, I glossed the notion of a *possible world* as a way the actual world could have been. This is fine, as far as it goes, provided we keep thinking in terms of a *complete* way the actual world could have been. My being six inches taller than I am is not a possible world – it's just a possible state of affairs. Presumably, though, there *is* a possible world in which I am six inches taller than I actually am; that is, there is a complete and logically coherent world in which I am six inches taller (I *think* this is a possible world). What is supposed to be so cool about the terminology of possible worlds is that it gives us a rich vocabulary for talking and thinking about possibility and necessity more generally. For example, we can now think of necessary truths as those that are true in *every* possible world (i.e., there is no way the world could have been such that they would have been false). Similarly, if something is impossible, then we can say that it occurs in no possible world (i.e., there is no way the world could have been such that this thing would have occurred). Thus, $2 + 2 = 4$ is true in every possible world, and round squares occur in no possible world.

Now, let's think about God's creative activity in terms of possible worlds. When (if?) God created the universe we find ourselves in, one possible world was instantiated. But God did not create the possible world – after all, a possible world is an abstract object, like the number 7 or a triangle, and God doesn't create such things.[13] Before God made anything at all, we might say, all the possible worlds were already "there" waiting to be considered by God as candidates for creation.[14]

In creating, God *actualizes* one of these possible worlds. If we follow the Genesis account, God speaks the heavens and the earth into existence. In doing so, God thereby makes it the case that a particular possible world has an actual instance.

With these thoughts in mind, return to the tempting idea we are attributing to Mackie. It can now be put this way: God, being omnipotent, can actualize any possible world. According to Plantinga, this may be false. To think that it must be true, he claims, is to fall prey to what he calls "Leibniz's Lapse."

In order to see this lapse, return to the free will story from which we extracted (C). On this story, human beings are free – free in what philosophers have come to call the "libertarian" sense. A libertarian about free will thinks that this freedom is incompatible with antecedent determination. That is, the libertarian thinks, roughly, that if a person's action is determined by something prior to her own decision, then the action is not an expression of free will. Put another way, if anything other than the person herself guarantees that she does one thing rather than another, then she is not free in this libertarian sense. This has an important implication for God's creative activity. If God wants to bring about a world that contains free creatures of the sort we have just described, then the creative process cannot antecedently determine what these beings will do – otherwise, the beings will not in fact be free.

Recall, now, the possible world that Mackie thinks God ought to have actualized. This is a world containing free creatures and all of the goods contingent upon freedom, but in which every one of these creatures uses his or her freedom well: a world in which none of these free creatures chooses wrongly. It is important to continue to emphasize that Plantinga does not deny that there *is* such a possible world. A world like the one for which Mackie pleads is broadly logically possible. But God may *still* not be able to actualize it, omnipotence notwithstanding. Consider two different senses of what it would mean to actualize this world – a strong sense and a weak sense. To strongly actualize this world would simply be to cause it to be actual, to make it so, as it were. But God cannot strongly actualize this world because then there would be a condition sufficient for the agents' choices in it that preceded their choices. In other words, simply making this world would entail eliminating all the free will in it.

What about this weaker sense of actualization? Well, to weakly actualize this world would be to cause everything to be actual that would be necessary for the world to have all of these free creatures acting well with their freedom. So, if God weakly actualizes a world in which I freely choose to tell the truth, then this is a matter of God's making me and the world such that I am in position to use my freedom at the relevant time to tell the truth. But, again, God can't *make* me tell the truth and still have me do so freely. So everything that God does in weakly actualizing a world in which I freely tell the truth in a certain situation is exactly the same as what God does in weakly actualizing a world in which I freely lie in that same situation. Here comes the rub, then. Suppose I freely tell the truth in the situation. Then there is a world that God could *not* have weakly actualized (even though it was a logically possible one): namely, one in which I freely lie. Of course, God could simply cause me to lie, but then I wouldn't be lying freely. On the other hand, suppose I freely lie in the situation. Then there is a world that God could not have weakly actualized: namely, one in which I freely tell the truth. Again, God could simply cause me to tell the truth, but then I wouldn't be acting freely in doing so. In either case, then, there is a possible world that not even an omnipotent being can bring about while still preserving my freedom. What this appears to show is that Leibniz really was lapsing and Mackie really was making a mistake when each of them accepted the conclusion that God could actualize any world that happened to strike the divine fancy. Contrary to these esteemed gentlemen, it does not necessarily follow from the fact that a certain state of affairs is logically possible that an omnipotent being can bring it about.

2.6   Getting Depraved

The defense is not yet complete, however. Even if we grant that there are some possible worlds that not even an omnipotent being can actualize, it doesn't follow that there is a particular problem with the world Mackie wants. Here we come to another place in Plantinga's argument at which misunderstanding of the logical and argumentative situation has led interpreters of it down a wrong path, for it is at this point that Plantinga invokes the infamous possibility of *Transworld Depravity*. As he characterizes it, a person is transworld depraved if she would do something morally wrong in *any* possible world in which she was actualized. With this in mind, Plantinga asks us to imagine the possibility that everyone (every actual and every possible person) suffers from transworld depravity. Taken as a doctrinal commitment, universal transworld depravity would be a deeply counterintuitive and unmotivated one. But Plantinga does not characterize and appeal to transworld depravity as a commitment at all, doctrinal or otherwise. His crucial point here has to do with *logical possibility*.

Let's keep our eyes on the dialectical prize. Plantinga has invoked the possibility that proposition (C) is true in order to demonstrate that the theistic set is not formally inconsistent. A crucial component of (C) is the claim that it was impossible for God to create a world containing free creatures that did not also contain evil. If it is so much as *possible* that (C) is true, then Plantinga will have found a possibly-true proposition consistent with (1)–(4) of the theistic set that entails (5); and he will have shown thereby, *contra* Mackie, that accepting the theistic set need not involve contradicting oneself. I re-emphasize all of this to help us see why the appeal to the bare logical possibility of universal transworld depravity is all that Plantinga needs for his argument. If it is logically possible that everyone is transworld depraved, then it is logically possible that there was no way for God to actualize a world containing free creatures that did not also contain evil. Does Plantinga believe that all of us suffer from transworld depravity? No! He may not even think that there is a single person so unfortunate. He thinks only that complete transworld depravity is *possible*. If it is, then (C) remains possibly true – even though the sinless world Mackie invokes also remains a logically possible one. If (C) is possibly true, then (1)–(5) can all be true together, and the free will defense is nearly complete.

All we need now to finish up with Plantinga's defense are some *pro forma* responses to potential objections. Plantinga takes up two of these in particular. First, we might want to know what the free will defense can say about the *amount* of evil we find in the world. The challenge here might be put like this: even if the existence of some evil is consistent with propositions (1)–(4) of the theistic set, the sheer volume of evil may not be. A second potential objection might be formulated not in terms of the amount but rather in terms of one particular *kind* of evil we find in the world – what we often refer to as "natural" evil. Once again, to appreciate Plantinga's especially quick handling of these objections, we have to keep in mind the logical structure of the free will defense. As we will see in the next chapters, the amount and kinds of evil are real problems for the rationality of theistic belief. But they really are not much problem *here* – namely, for the free will defense in response to the logical problem of evil. This is because, in this context, Plantinga has only to show the *bare logical possibility* that God could not have created a world with free creatures in it that did not contain these amounts and kinds of evil.

With respect to the amount of evil, there is surely something to the thought that it would have been easy for an omnipotent being to create a world with slightly less evil and just as much good. We could easily imagine our own world with a couple hundred fewer murders per year, for example, or with less child abuse and greedy consumption. Fair enough. As easy as this might be to imagine, however, it is also possible – just *possible* – that our imaginations are leading us astray here. To highlight this possibility, bring before your mind all of the possible worlds with free creatures in them that contain as much good as our own and less evil. In such worlds, we must presume, the free creatures use their freedom somewhat better than the free creatures do in the actual world. However, since the creatures in these alternative worlds were indeed free, it was not possible for God simply to *cause* one of these worlds to exist; God could not strongly actualize such a world, since that would involve undermining free will. Once again, God could only weakly actualize such a world – that is, create the circumstances in which these creatures were given the opportunity to make better choices than the ones that have been made in the actual world. Still, if the world God weakly actualizes turns out better than this one, it will be because the free creatures in this alternative world used their freedom better. In essence, it will be because the creatures were more cooperative with God in the alternative world than they have turned out to be in this one. But does logic require all of the creatures in any of these potentially better worlds to use their freedom better? Isn't it possible – just *possible* – that some of the creatures in these potentially better worlds are deeply uncooperative, so that for every possible world that is better than the actual one, there are some free creatures who fail to use their freedom in such a way that the better world is in fact actualized? It seems so. This would mean that it is possibly true that even though there *are* better possible worlds, it is not possible for God to actualize any of them.

With respect to the special kind of evil we call "natural" evil, Plantinga makes a similar point. Natural evil is supposed to be distinguishable from moral evil largely in that the latter can reasonably be attributed to bad free choices, while the former cannot be. Murder, theft, lying, and the consequences of these things look to be the result of bad free choices. By contrast, however, a great deal of suffering comes about by way of tornadoes, hurricanes, animal predation, and the like of these – none of which, it would seem, have much to do with the sort of free will to which the free will defender appeals. This might suggest a problem for the free will defense. Again, however, this problem is easy to parry. Since we need only a bare logical possibility, here's one that will work. It is logically possible that all of the so-called natural evil we find in the world is the result of the free choices of nonhuman (but very powerful) agents. The various theistic traditions share the idea of the existence of such agents in the form of Satan or demons. Perhaps, then, even natural evil is really a species of moral evil because it, too, has bad free choices – of these demonic agents – as its source. With this thought in mind, it isn't hard to re-apply all of the prior argumentation about the implications of human freedom for what worlds God may not be able to actualize. (More harping on the logical structure here. Does Plantinga think that Satan is the cause of all natural evil? Of course not. He thinks only that this is a logical possibility, which is all he needs for the argument.)

The conclusion seems now quite firmly established. By appealing to a robust conception of free will, Plantinga appears to have demonstrated that the logical argument from evil fails. He concludes: "[i]f evil is a problem for the believer, it is not that the existence of evil – moral or natural – is inconsistent with the existence of God" (1990, 109).

2.7 Going Deeper: Incompatibilism

In my presentation of the logical problem of evil, I have tried to communicate the (somewhat surprising) general consensus of the philosophical community that Plantinga's free will defense is decisively successful. At the very least, as I said above, it is worth attending to its supposed success as an intriguing sociological fact. And we are now in position to appreciate, as some further evidence for the sociological claim, William Alston's conclusion that "Plantinga…has established the *possibility* that God could not actualize a world containing free creatures that always do the right thing" (1996, 113). As we turn to a few strategies of response to the free will defense, flying as they are in the face of the consensus, we can use the content of Alston's assertion as our foil. This is to say that those who wish to resist Plantinga's argument will need to show that it does *not* establish the possibility (not even the broadly logical possibility) that Alston claims it does.

An initial effort to show this might take its lead from William Rowe's concession to the fundamental force of Plantinga's argument. Rowe echoes Alston, writing:

> Some philosophers have contended that the existence of evil is logically inconsistent with the existence of the theistic God. No one, I think, has succeeded in establishing such an extravagant claim. Indeed, *granted incompatibilism*, there is a fairly compelling argument for the view that the existence of evil is logically consistent with the existence of the theistic God. (For a lucid statement of this argument, see Alvin Plantinga, *God, Freedom, and Evil.*) (1996, 10 n. 1; emphasis added)

So, in addition to giving considerable deference to Plantinga's argument, Rowe also indicates an important direction in which opponents of the free will defense might move. Notice, in particular, the bit of Rowe's quote that I have italicized. Rowe appears to be allowing that the compelling nature of the free will defense is contingent upon the acceptance of incompatibilism. This is worth exploring, especially since a number of the earliest efforts to block the free will defense launched attacks at just this point.

We should remind ourselves that incompatibilism is the thesis that free will is incompatible with external determination. If what a person does is determined by anything outside her own will (by the past and laws of nature, for example, or by early childhood neurobiology, or by God's intentions), then she does not do it freely. Thus, on this conception, in order for a person to perform a free act, it must be true of her at the time she acts that, holding everything fixed about her and the world, she could either perform the act or refrain from performing the act. Free will, then, is understood to be a genuine two-way power. Obviously, this is crucial to Plantinga's free will defense. If incompatibilism is false, then this means it is possible for a person to act freely even when her action is determined in advance by pre-existing conditions. In other words, it will seem that there's no reason to suppose that God could not have causally determined the world to unfold so that everyone does only what is right and good – and this *without* sacrificing free will and all the good things it makes possible.

Mackie himself mounted some initial effort to deflate the free will defense here. After a brief explanation of the appeal to free will in response to his argument, Mackie begins his dismissal with this: "I think that this solution is unsatisfactory primarily because of the incoherence of the notion of freedom of will: but I cannot discuss this topic adequately here" (1955, 33). Similarly, Antony Flew takes his stand against the free will defense by attacking "the idea that there is a contradiction involved in saying that God might have made people so that they always in fact *freely* chose right" (1955, 149). Both Mackie and Flew (and many others in this heyday of neo-Humean positivism) were convinced compatibilists. We shouldn't be surprised, given not only their commitment to compatibilism but what they took to be the utter obviousness of compatibilism, that these early responses to the free will defense placed the edge of the dialectical sword here. Nor should we be surprised, I suppose, that the tone of argument on this point was mildly condescending.

We can take compatibilism to be the denial of incompatibilism. Thus, if compatibilism is true, then a person can enjoy free will even if she is determined by antecedent circumstances to do what she does. It turns out that compatibilism remains quite popular among contemporary philosophers.[15] Furthermore, I am myself an incompatibilist who concedes that recent developments of compatibilism are not without force and attraction.[16] But neither the popularity nor even the plausibility of compatibilism would be enough to vindicate a Mackie-style argument from evil. It would not be enough, after all, simply for compatibilism to be true. It must also be the case that incompatibilism is *necessarily* false. And this would be a very difficult thing for the proponent of the logical problem to show.

What is crucial to see here is, once again, the very high bar the proponent of the logical problem must get over. The height at which this bar has been set (and set, let me remind us, by the aspirations of the argument itself) is intimated already in Mackie's first response. Mackie thinks the relevant notion of free will is *incoherent*. Notice, however, that nothing less than incoherence will do. This is because the free will defender still needs only the bare logical possibility that God could not have created a world containing moral good without also creating a world containing moral evil – and therefore only the bare logical possibility of the truth of incompatibilism. If incompatibilist free will is so much as logically possible, then the defense will run through.

Can it be shown that the incompatibilist conception of free will (libertarianism) on which the free will defense depends is incoherent or in some sense logically impossible? If it can be, it is somewhat surprising that even quite forceful critics of libertarianism stop short of doing so – and are in fact explicit about the limitations here. Consider, for example, the influential and skeptical views of both Derk Pereboom and Randolph Clarke. They share the view that agent-causalism is the most promising version of libertarianism.[17] They also share the view that there is not very much promise here. Nevertheless, it is interesting to note the different grounds of their respective skepticisms.

On Pereboom's view, agent-causal libertarianism runs into trouble with our scientific view of the world. Specifically, he claims that libertarian agency theory is

> seriously challenged by empirical considerations. The main problem for this position is that our choices produce physical events in the brain and in the rest of the body, and these events seem to be governed by physical laws. The agent-causal libertarian must make it credible that our actions can be freely willed in the sense it advocates given the evidence we have about these physical laws. I argue that given this evidence, it is doubtful that our actions can be freely willed in the sense the agent-causal view proposes. (2004, xvi)

This is to say that, by Pereboom's lights, libertarianism is in a bad evidential position. He goes to considerable lengths to insist that the agent-causal variety of libertarianism in particular is *not*, however, straightforwardly incoherent. Rather, the problems for libertarianism emerge at the level of empirical investigation. After laying these problems out in detail, Pereboom concludes: "If the arguments I have presented here are sound, one should be skeptical about the prospects of libertarianism" (2004, 88).

Clarke's conclusions are similarly restrained, if slightly more pessimistic. In part, this somewhat more pointed pessimism is due to the fact that Clarke feels the force of some objections to agent-causal libertarianism that are not merely empirical in nature. Some of these concerns, he recognizes, have the potential to threaten the coherence of agent-causation. Still, notice the healthy tentativeness of the conclusions he draws from his considerations:

> Although none of these considerations is individually decisive, collectively, it seems to me, they incline the balance against the possibility of substance causation in general and agent-causation in particular. There are, on balance, reasons to think that agent causation, as affirmed by an agent-causal account of free will, is impossible.

> However, any case against agent causation is attenuated by the difficulty we encounter in understanding causation. Just what causation is and how it works *in any case* is hard to say. Hence, we cannot have a *great deal* of confidence in the claims made here to the effect that it cannot work in the way an agent-causal theory of free will requires. We should doubt the possibility of agent causation, but we should not be very certain about the matter. (2005, 209–10; emphasis in original)

According to Clarke, agent causation is, then, *probably impossible*. And notice that Clarke's restraint appears to have two sources. First, he recognizes that the initial impossibility determination rests on a "balancing" argument that is delicate in its own right. Second, the issues are so complex and difficult that only hubris could make confident pronouncements about the conclusions we should draw about them.

On my view, Pereboom and Clarke are giving us the most sensible and carefully argued skeptical views about libertarian free will in the contemporary discussion.[18] And notice that as skeptical as these views are, they do not appear to be quite skeptical enough to give the opponent of Plantinga's free will defense much succor. In Pereboom's case, there is simply no incoherence in the neighborhood with regard to libertarianism. For Clarke, while incoherence is in the neighborhood, he does not urge us to accept it with the kind of force that would be necessary to undermine the broadly logical possibility on which this response to the logical problem of evil rests.[19]

2.8 Going Still Deeper: Transworld Depravity

Another recent effort to undo the free will defense has come from some who worry that universal transworld depravity is not so clearly logically possible as Plantinga assumed. We should be careful to see here that the proper complaint, if there is one, is not about it being *implausible* that everyone is transworld depraved or about how silly the concept of such depravity is. Since universal transworld depravity needs only to be *possible* in order for the free will defense to succeed, the complaint must be that the concept is, in some respect, impossible to instantiate. It is also interesting to note that those who have pressed this concern most forcefully are, as a general rule, largely in sympathy with the broad outlines of the free will defense. Thus, while they raise this sort of concern for Plantinga's specific argument, they are inclined to think that, with some appropriate modifications, a version of the free will defense will succeed.

Keith DeRose, for example, has argued that the second stage of Plantinga's defense does not advance the argument because our modal intuitions about the possibility of universal transworld depravity are too unclear (1991). Daniel Howard-Snyder and John Hawthorne have given this sort of concern some sharper teeth by bringing out an implication of the possibility of universal transworld depravity (1998). If it is possible that every potential person is transworld depraved, then it is impossible for there to be any person who is "transworld sanctified." A person is transworld sanctified if, very roughly, she would never do wrong in any situation in which God might place her (and in which God gives her significant freedom). As Howard-Snyder and Hawthorne point out, it is not terribly unnatural to think that it is at least possible that there is someone for whom it is necessarily true that he or she is transworld sanctified. However, since universal transworld depravity is incompatible with individual transworld sanctity, at most one of these is really possible. That is, either

(TWD) Every potential person is transworld depraved

or

(NTWS) Necessarily, some potential person is transworld sanctified

is possible, but not both.[20] The conclusion they draw is that we have no good reason to prefer one of these modal commitments to the other. In essence, then, we should ultimately withhold judgment about the possibility of universal transworld depravity. If we do so, then Plantinga's defense, as it stands, is not a demonstrative success. We ought, it seems, to remain agnostic about its success.[21]

However, Howard-Snyder and Hawthorne go on to accommodate their point into a "Plantinga-style" defense that they do believe succeeds. To do this, all that is needed is a small shift in argumentative focus. In Plantinga's presentation of his defense, he insisted, without argument, that universal transworld depravity is possible. But he didn't need even this much to counter the logical problem of evil. Holding everything else in the defense fixed, Howard-Snyder and Hawthorne argue that all that is needed (for what they refer to as a bare epistemic defense) is that *for all we know* or *for all we have reason to believe* universal transworld depravity is possible. This keeps the burden of proof where it surely lies – with the Mackie-style arguer who is attempting to show us that the theistic set is inconsistent. The defender needs neither to insist nor to demonstrate that universal transworld depravity is possible. It is enough that it is possible *for all we have reason to believe.* Of course, it remains open to the defender of the logical problem to show that it is, in fact, not possible. But the prospects for this project are not promising.[22]

2.9 Conclusion

Where does all of this leave us? I think it is reasonable to conclude from this rich and pointed debate that the logical problem of evil can be parried. As challenging as Mackie's argument is, it is precisely its argumentative boldness that ultimately leaves it vulnerable. By overreaching to charge the theist with incoherence, proponents of the logical problem of evil have made it surprisingly easy to resist. Frankly, once we understand the challenge, it isn't very difficult for the theist to conjure up broadly logical possibilities (consistent with theism) that would make the theistic set consistent.

The complex and rigorous machinery of the second stage of Plantinga's free will defense may give the impression that only such carefully constructed arguments will do the work of blocking the logical problem. But this isn't so. On my view, the real genius and value of Plantinga's highly developed counterargument is to be found in the way that it lays bare both the logic of the problem and the remarkably delicate dialectical requirements of its success. Thus, even if one or another of the challenges to the details of Plantinga's free will defense turns out to have force, then, as with Howard-Snyder and Hawthorne, we can now see that small but acceptable modifications will be able to be made. Furthermore, Plantinga famously made it harder on himself by assuming that God knows what each of us would freely do in any circumstance in which we might be placed.[23] Suppose this very controversial view is false (as I think it is, by the way). Suppose, for example, that what a free being will do in some circumstance is sometimes antecedently indeterminate – so that not even God knows what the being will do in advance of his doing it.[24] Then God cannot sensibly be envisioned as creating a world like ours by selecting among complete possible worlds fully presented to the divine mind in advance of creation. Thanks to Plantinga, we now know that a defense in response to the logical problem needs to show the bare logical possibility that God could not have made a world with moral good without also making a world containing moral evil. If not even God knows in advance how free beings will use their freedom, then while it may be broadly logically possible for the world to contain such beings who always choose rightly, God would have no way of knowing, in advance of creating, that this would be so. God, that is, may have to take a risk in creating free beings like ourselves – a risk that necessarily entails the possibility of free wrongdoing on the part of creatures. If something like this were possible, then we would have reason to think that the crucial compatibility premise (C) is possibly true, and this without needing to chastise Leibniz for his lapse or invoke the controversial possibility of universal transworld depravity. In short, then, if Plantinga's free will defense is not as decisive a success as many contemporary philosophers have supposed (and it still may be), at the very least it provides the crucial foundation for many others that are successful.

The bad news for the theist, however, is that this does not put an end to the problem of evil. In fact, it was precisely in response to the supposed success of Plantinga's reply to the logical problem of evil that contemporary philosophers of religion turned their attention to developing a version of the problem that is much harder to dismiss than Mackie's. This is the subject of our next chapter.

3
The Evidential Problem

Having wrestled with the logical version of the problem of evil in the last chapter, I wouldn't blame you for worrying that philosophers have been distracted by the trees in their search for the forest. The logic-chopping and modal semantics into which we wandered before can, I grant, seem too abstract – too bloodless – to be at the heart of our concerns about evil. And I will admit that it is hard to envision either Ivan Karamazov or Dostoevsky's "ridiculous man" having much patience with the details and import of transworld depravity. Still, we should proceed cautiously here. I wouldn't blame you for *worrying* about the abstract nature of our earlier discussion; but I do not, in the end, think that the abstraction and rigorous logical reasoning are a distraction. Unfortunately, they simply cannot be avoided if we hope to make progress on these issues. What I am willing to admit, then, is that a responsible assessment of the logical argument from evil for atheism (getting the argument into a forceful shape and appreciating the best responses to it) requires us to think very hard about issues that can seem a long way from our point of departure. This does not mean, however, that I am willing to admit that we shouldn't have taken the journey or that we should have turned back earlier. As I see the matter, there was no easier way through the terrain. The problems of evil, I'm afraid, are just very hard.

Now, in a sense, the central arguments of this chapter are less abstract and theoretical than those we faced in the previous chapter. The evidential problem of evil, unlike its logical sibling, is premised on concrete, real-world cases of suffering, cases often presented in considerable gritty detail. This might assuage some worries about the putative distance between philosophical reflection and common thinking on these issues. We will not, however, be able to escape the demands of rigorous philosophy – not, at least, if we genuinely hope to think to the bottom of things in this domain and have robustly warranted beliefs about the relationship between theism and evil. If the logical problem pressed us more deeply into the metaphysics of modality than we might have expected, the evidential problem will do the same with respect to some fundamental issues in epistemology and value theory.

As it turns out, there are actually quite a few versions of the evidential argument from evil for atheism, only one of which will we look at carefully in this chapter. As with the logical argument, the details matter and grasping them will demand our focused attention. Fortunately, the general intuitive ideas animating evidential versions of the argument from evil can be given a gripping initial presentation. The core thought is that the existence of evil – and here we mean evil in all its actual horrific amounts and forms – is *good evidence* that the God of common theism does not exist. Thus, whereas a Mackie-style deductive argument from evil attempts to demonstrate that the existence of God is logically incompatible with the existence of evil, the evidential versions of the argument (in their strongest forms) hope to establish the (nevertheless weaker) claim that the existence of the specific evils we find in the world makes the existence of God unlikely or makes it epistemically unreasonable to believe that God exists.

An analogy may help here. Suppose you see a toddler wandering, apparently unmonitored, around an amusement park. You begin to wonder if the child really is unmonitored or if, rather, the child's parent is watching providentially from a distance, perhaps hidden in the crowd or just out of your view. Now suppose that you watch the child stumble into the path of a go-cart that runs painfully over the child's foot. As the child screams in pain, tears flowing, no parent appears. This would seem to be very strong evidence either that the parent is not around or that the parent is not good. Notice that the existence and goodness of the parent is not *logically incompatible* with what we've seen. We can imagine a possible situation in which, for example, the parent is present and would have appeared on scene if he could, but was at just that time saving his other child from the sure death of falling over the edge of a precipice (an amusement park can be a dangerous place!). So it is *possible* that a good parent is present even though the child we are watching ends up both hurt and uncomforted. Still, we take what we have seen as strong evidence that a good parent isn't around. It may even seem to be unreasonable, under these conditions, to believe otherwise. In the same way, the proponents of evidential arguments for atheism take the evils we find in the world as similarly strong evidence that the universe is not being overseen by a maximally good God, even if they also accept (as most do) that the existence of God is not *logically* incompatible with the world's evils.

With this motivational sketch of the evidential argument in place, we can now turn to the most influential and widely discussed version of it.

3.1 William Rowe's Evidential Argument

In the last chapter, we took notice of William Rowe's willingness to grant that Plantinga's free will defense silences the logical problem of evil. In granting this, however, Rowe went on to formulate a version of the problem that cannot be dismissed by appealing to the bare logical possibilities mustered by the free will defender. It is fair to say that Rowe has done for the evidential argument from evil what Mackie did for the logical argument. And just as Mackie's article "Evil and Omnipotence" can be regarded as the source of the contemporary debate over the logical problem of evil, so Rowe's article "The Problem of Evil and Some Varieties of Atheism" (1979) has set the agenda for discussion of the evidential problem. In this article and in a number of others, Rowe has given the evidential argument an especially crisp and penetrating presentation that continues to be the touchstone of the ongoing debate. Since Rowe's thinking about the evidential problem has gone through some transformations over the decades, it is somewhat misleading to attribute *one* argument to Rowe.[1] Still, the core elements have stayed fixed and the central appeal of the strategy has remained substantially unchanged since 1979. I propose, then, to treat Rowe's contributions as the development of a single line of forceful reasoning. I hope that what will be lost in terms of technical precision in taking this approach will be regained in accessibility and ease of presentation.

Rowe seeks to animate his evidential argument by drawing our attention to particular instances of horrible suffering. Typically, his argument is accompanied by the following two cases:

> E1: A fawn is trapped in a forest fire. Unable to escape, the fawn is badly burned but not immediately killed. Instead, the fawn lies in excruciating pain on the forest floor for a number of days until it finally succumbs to the trauma of its burns.
>
> E2: A five-year-old girl in Flint, Michigan is brutally beaten, raped, and strangled to death by her mother's boyfriend on New Year's Day, 1986.[2]

Now, keep in mind that while Rowe has carefully chosen these cases (E1 is a construction of Rowe's imagination, while E2 is based on an actual news story) to make it difficult for the theist to explain them away by appeal to some or another standard justification, they are not supposed to be especially unusual. Situations like those described, Rowe would want us to remember, are all too common. When we consider the history of the world, we are sadly forced to admit that scenes of the kind depicted in E1 and E2 are widespread and disturbingly numerous.

With these kinds of concrete suffering (and some sensitivity to their amount) clearly before our minds, we are ready for Rowe's formal argument. It goes like this:

1. There are instances of intense suffering (like those described in E1 and E2) which an omnipotent, omniscient being could have prevented without thereby losing some greater

good or permitting some evil equally bad or worse. [Call this the "Empirical Premise" (EP) and note that it can be glossed as the claim that that there are gratuitous evils.]

2. An omniscient, wholly good being would prevent the occurrence of any intense suffering it could, unless it could not do so without thereby losing some greater good or permitting some evil equally bad or worse. [Call this the "Theological Premise" (TP) and note that it can be glossed as the claim that if God exists, then there are no gratuitous evils.]
3. Therefore, there does not exist an omnipotent, omniscient, wholly good being. (1967, 118–30)

Once we clarify some terminology, we will be able to appreciate the points I have put in brackets above. So, notice that the first premise is making something of an empirical assertion: the world contains evils of a particular sort. Of what sort? Of the sort such that a being with God's powers could have prevented them at no net moral cost. If we follow the custom of calling an evil that God could have prevented at no net moral cost "gratuitous," then premise 1 asserts that there are gratuitous evils, as I say in the brackets. The second premise makes a conceptual or theological claim. It expresses the thought that a being with God's character would tolerate an evil only if preventing it would have a net moral cost. This is to say that if God exists, then there are no gratuitous evils, as I say in the brackets.

A word about the structure of this argument. As it stands, it has the form of a valid deductive argument. What makes this argument "evidential" – or sometimes "inductive" – is the fact that EP, the first premise, is not taken to be a demonstrated truth (TP, the second premise, may not be as secure as it has typically been thought to be either, but let's save that for now). Instead, the empirical premise needs ultimately to be supported by a kind of evidence or argument that even Rowe himself grants will not constitute "proof." The reasoning Rowe deploys in defense of the empirical premise turns out to be the subject of considerable controversy; we will turn to it soon enough. For now, though, what is important to see is that, given this argument's valid form, it seems that we should be as committed to the conclusion as we are to the premises. That is, if we have strong reasons to accept the premises, then we will have equally strong reasons to accept the conclusion.

It will also be important to attend to the somewhat limited *aim* of Rowe's argument. What Rowe hopes to show by offering it is that the existence of evils like E1 and E2 is strong evidence for atheism. But one particular set of considerations can be strong evidence for a thesis even if, all things considered, the thesis should be rejected. This is because there might be further evidence unrelated to the original supporting considerations that militate powerfully against the thesis. If Rowe's argument succeeds, then, what it shows is that *on the assumption that we have no independent arguments for theism*, we should conclude that God does not exist. The bit in italics is crucial because it puts the argument in its proper context. As an evidential argument, it purports to provide evidence for its conclusion but not to establish it decisively. In other words, Rowe takes himself to be showing that, "putting aside whatever reasons there may be to think that the theistic God exists, the facts about evil in our world provide good reason to think that God does not exist" (Howard-Snyder et al. 2001, 136). What this means is that, strictly speaking, the theist could, as we will see in more detail later, simply accept the reasonability of the premises of Rowe's argument but go on to claim that the positive evidence for theism outweighs the negative evidence constituted by the existence of apparently gratuitous evil.

3.2 Defending the Premises

But why should we accept Rowe's premises, EP and TP? Are there good grounds for doing so? Let's begin with TP since, as I hinted above, it has faced the lightest objections. Presumably, you can see why it has been generally accepted. According to the theological premise, God would not permit evils like E1 and E2 unless there were overriding reasons to do so. This is supposed to be supported by *a priori* reasoning about the nature of perfect goodness and knowledge. If a being permits an instance of intense suffering without an overriding reason, then this being trades the better (avoiding the intense suffering) for the worse (whatever it would have cost to avoid the suffering).[3] But a being can trade the better for the worse only if the being is not wholly good or the being is ignorant of the costs of the trade. Thus, an omnibenevolent and omniscient being can permit evils like E1 and E2 only if there is an overriding reason to do so. Since it is the absence of such overriding reasons that would make such evils gratuitous, an omnibenevolent and omniscient being will not permit gratuitous evils. That is, if God exists, then there are no such evils.

EP is much trickier to defend, as you might imagine. According to this empirical premise, there are in fact evils that occur in our world that an omniscient and omnipotent being could have prevented at no net moral cost. There are, Rowe claims here in the first premise, instances of intense suffering that a being like God would have had an overriding reason to prevent. The challenge, however, should be clear. Echoing an important line of objection to Rowe's argument, it would be natural to wonder how we could know that a particular instance of intense suffering, like E1 or E2, is not tolerated for some overriding reason. How could we be justified in believing that some such evils could have been prevented at no net moral cost? It is important to see that Rowe is initially sensitive to this problem. He does not think, for example, that is *impossible* that there are overriding reasons for the permission of each of the instances of horrible suffering the world contains. However, he does think that we nevertheless have *good grounds* to accept that there are no such overriding reasons: good grounds, that is, to accept the first premise of his argument.

And now we are at the controversial heart of the argument. What Rowe claims is that *our inability to see* any good reasons God could have for permitting E1 and E2 (and the countless similar cases we encounter all the time[4]) justifies us in concluding *that there are no* good reasons. This is a natural and reasonable form of inference in many contexts. From my inability to see x, it is frequently quite reasonable to conclude that there is no x. For example, from my inability to see the book I'm looking for on my desk I can reasonably conclude that it is not on my desk. From your inability to see your friend in the room you can reasonably conclude that she's not in the room. And this form of inference certainly can apply to our search for reasons, too. My inability to see what good reason my son could have for eating dirt licenses my inference that there is no good reason. Your inability to ascertain a good reason that your co-worker has for treating you badly licenses your conclusion that he has no good reason. Rowe contends that this form of inference can structure a forceful argument for his empirical first premise, EP. Specifically, he claims that

> (P) No good we know of justifies an omnipotent, omniscient, and wholly good being in permitting E1 and E2

gives us very good grounds for accepting

> (Q) No good at all justifies an omnipotent, omniscient, and wholly good being in permitting E1 and E2 (note that Q is identical to EP, premise 1).

Now, remember that Rowe has carefully selected E1 and E2 so as to make it very difficult to see what good reasons a being with God's attributes could have for permitting them. For example, the appeal to the value of free will isn't going to help, it seems, with the fawn's suffering in E1, since it is hard to see how this event could be crucial to preserving some important form of freedom. The traditional appeal to the value of moral and/or spiritual maturation (traditionally called "soul-building") falls similarly flat when we consider E2, since it doesn't make much sense to claim that the little girl's suffering could contribute to her development – after all, she's in no position to take anything away from it other than pain and terror, and she dies almost immediately. Furthermore, even if we can cook up a willingness to see some good in the freedom exercised by the boyfriend and in the soul-building made possible by the fawn's agony, many of us are powerfully inclined to think that these goods do not outweigh the deep suffering in both cases. What Rowe claims, then, is that "[w]hen we reflect on some good we know of we can see that it is likely, if not certain, that the good in question *either* is not good enough to justify God in permitting E1 and E2 *or* is such that an omnipotent, omniscient being could realize it (or some greater good) without having to permit E1 or E2" (1996, 276–7). In other words, Rowe takes himself to be on solid ground in asserting P.

The remaining question, then, is whether we should accept the inference of Q from P – call this *Rowe's Inference*. If it is reasonable to accept *Rowe's Inference*, then the empirical premise will have reasonable support. That is, we will have good reason to think that there are in fact gratuitous evils. As we will see, the dispute over *Rowe's Inference* has been both deep and wide, but we should now be able to see the considerable power of his argument.

3.3 Resisting EP

Rowe's empirical first premise (EP) has generally been thought to be the point of principal vulnerability in his argument. It makes sense, then, for us to begin with responses to Rowe's argument that take aim at EP. We should notice, however, two different ways that an objection to Rowe's argument could be aimed at EP. On the one hand, one might hope to demonstrate that EP is flatly false. That is, one might attempt to offer compelling reasons for thinking that there really are no gratuitous evils, appearances notwithstanding with respect to E1, E2, and the rest. On the other hand, one might hope to show not that EP is false but only that Rowe has given no good reason to think it is true. That is, one might attempt to resist Rowe's reasons for thinking that E1, E2, and the rest are gratuitous. To take up the first strategy would be to take up a project of theodicy. Remember that, as we are thinking of it, a project of theodicy involves an effort to identify a set of morally sufficient reasons God can plausibly be thought to have for permitting the evils in the world. If one or another version of this project succeeds, then EP will have thereby been shown to be false. Since we will be taking up the project of theodicy on its own terms in chapter 5, let's set this response to Rowe's argument to the side. Perhaps it is enough to recognize that if, in the end, the only way to avoid the argument is to construct a successful theodicy, then Rowe deserves considerable credit for having pressed the theist into an exceedingly unenviable dialectical position, and this even if the project of theodicy can ultimately succeed.

But the second way to target EP does not require the construction of a theodicy since it does not require the conclusion that EP is *false*. The opponent of Rowe's argument who takes up this second strategy need only identify compelling grounds for *withholding judgment* about EP. The most influential version of this strategy (and, indeed, perhaps the most influential general strategy of response to Rowe's argument) takes up a stance that has come to be known as *Skeptical Theism* (cf. Wykstra 1996; Alston 1996; Bergmann 2001; Plantinga 1988; van Inwagen 1991). We should be careful right from the outset to emphasize that these skeptical theists are *not* skeptical about theism. Far from it! Rather, they are theists who are skeptical about *Rowe's Inference* of Q from P. Insofar as this skepticism is justified, the skeptical theists will have their grounds for resisting Rowe's argument at its first premise.

Now, why doubt the inference of P from Q? To appreciate the doubt, Stephen Wykstra has helpfully called the particular kind of inference Rowe's argument requires a "noseeum" inference – as in, we no-see-'em, so probably they ain't there (or, it is reasonable to conclude that they ain't there). In general, a noseeum inference is at work when we reasonably conclude that something doesn't exist because we have looked for it and don't find it. But it is only *sometimes* reasonable to conclude that something doesn't exist after we have looked for it and don't find it. This is to say that noseeum inferences are only sometimes valid. To see that noseeum inferences are not always valid, proponents of skeptical theism have done some substantial trafficking in analogies. Consider the beginner at chess who cannot see what good could come from Kasparov's decision to surrender his queen. Should we conclude from the fact that the beginner can't see the long-term and complex results of a master's move that there probably is no such good? No. Or consider someone who draws the conclusion that there is no intelligent life outside our solar system on the basis of her careful perusal of the night sky over many years. Having seen no aliens, she concludes that there are none. Would we accept this as a reasonable form of inference under these conditions? Clearly not. What is going wrong in these cases? In the first, we recognize that the beginner's inability to see Kasparov's plan would be at least as well explained by his ignorance of chess nuance as by the absence of good chess strategy on Kasparov's part. In the second case, we recognize that the terrain of the universe is so vast and uncharted and our faculties so limited that we have little reason to think that watching the night sky would be an effective way to reach conclusions about possible deep space denizens. In short, in these sorts of cases we have good reason to doubt that the agents in question *have what it takes* to get to the truth in the particular domain. Reflection on cases like these leads the skeptical theist to conclude that a noseeum inference of this form

> We haven't found any x's – so, there probably aren't any x's

is valid only if, under the circumstances, had there been some x's, we would probably have found them. In other words, good noseeum inferences presuppose that we would have been able to see-'em if they had been there.

As a way of seeing into the beating heart of skeptical theism, then, consider what would have to be true in order for Rowe's noseeum move from P to Q to be reasonable – presumably something like:

> (GOODS) If there were goods that would justify an omnipotent, omniscient, and wholly good being in permitting E1 and E2, then we would probably know about them.

The skeptical theist resists Rowe's Inference primarily because she is skeptical about the truth of (GOODS); that is, she is skeptical about the claim that we should have some confidence in our human abilities to gain epistemic access to the sorts of justifications available to God (if God exists). The intuitive idea behind the skeptical theist's epistemic humility in this domain is likely clear enough. Indeed, it is initially tempting to think that only epistemic hubris could provoke us to conclude that we are probably in a position to recognize the values to which *the divine ground of all being* could appeal in justifying the permission of horrendous evils. It is tempting, in short, to think that any confidence in (GOODS) is unwarranted.

Thinking about the vast possibilities for value beyond our ken and of the infinite vistas of concern that could be accessible to omniscient omnibenevolence, there seem to be *prima facie* good reasons to refuse to accept (GOODS). In the spirit of the analogies above (regarding chess and aliens), a further influential analogy can put us in the frame of mind to resist Rowe's particular noseeum inference. Consider the parent who must submit her four-year-old child to a painful procedure for the child's medical well-being. We do not expect the child to be able to understand the complex goods and evils (of long life, of cancer and chemotherapy, etc.), reflection on which animate the parent. If there are goods that justify the parent in permitting the horror of, say, chemotherapy (and, at least in some cases, there surely are), is it true that a four-year-old would probably know about them? Quite clearly no. All the skeptical theist appears to need in addition to this image, then, is the very compelling thought that our human epistemic situation before God would be sufficiently like the child's epistemic situation before her parent.

All of this looks to give the skeptical theist firm initial grounds for resisting (GOODS). And notice that the skeptical theist does *not* need to show that (GOODS) is false.[5] Proponents of Rowe's argument, if the above diagnosis is correct, bear the burden, rather, of showing that (GOODS) is plausibly thought to be true. The defensive posture of skeptical theism succeeds as long as striking it enables the theist to resist the considerations that Rowe and his consorts offer on behalf of the inferential move from P to Q.[6] What we should conclude, according to the skeptical theist, is that we have been given no good reason to accept the first premise (EP) of Rowe's evidential argument for atheism.

3.4   Resisting TP

The theological premise in Rowe's argument has generally been thought to be nearly unassailable; and we should admit

that the conceptual linkage between omniscient omnibenevolence and the justifiable permission of serious suffering must
be very tight. But TP insists that this linkage is *maximally*
tight. That is, TP tells us that the existence of God is *incompatible* with the existence of gratuitous evil. I grant that this
may be right. Maybe God would have to have an overridingly
good reason to allow any serious suffering. Still, I think it is
worth exploring the degree to which the force of this incompatibility claim might be weakened. A great deal here seems
to me to depend on disambiguating some different claims that
TP may be taken to express – and a great deal may also
depend on just what "omniscience" is taken to mean.

With respect to the disambiguations, return to the notion
of gratuitousness as it arises in Rowe's second premise; to
refresh our memories, this premise said:

2. An omniscient, wholly good being would prevent the
   occurrence of any intense suffering it could, unless it could
   not do so without thereby losing some greater good or
   permitting some evil equally bad or worse.

We can recall, also, that this led us to characterize gratuitous
evils as those that God could have prevented at no net moral
cost; that is, they are evils that God could have prevented
"without thereby losing some greater good or permitting
some evil equally bad or worse." But we can now see that
this is ambiguous between two different possible meanings of
gratuitousness:

(GE1) A particular instance of intense suffering e is a gratuitous evil if it is true that God could, *as a matter of fact*,
have prevented e without incurring a moral cost as high
as would have been incurred in permitting e itself.
(GE2) A particular instance of intense suffering e occurring
at t is a gratuitous evil if it is true that God could have
prevented e and God knew (or could reasonably have acted
on the supposition) at or before t that doing so would not
incur a moral cost as high as would have been incurred by
permitting e itself.

Recognizing the difference between GE1 and GE2 points us
to the possibility that the premises of Rowe's argument are

ambiguous in an important way; they are ambiguous between God's having what are sometimes called *absolute reasons* for permitting instances of evil versus God's having what are sometimes called *rationalizing reasons* for permitting instances of evil. Put roughly, God has an absolute reason to permit an instance of intense suffering if it is *true* that doing so would have no net moral cost. Equally roughly, God has a rationalizing reason to permit an instance of intense suffering if it is *reasonable for God to act on the supposition* that doing so would have no net moral cost. What GE1 shows us is that we might think of gratuitousness in terms of God's having no *absolute* reason to prevent an instance of evil, whereas GE2 shows us that we might think of gratuitousness in terms of God's having neither an *absolute* nor a *rationalizing* reason to prevent an instance of evil. I suspect that Rowe had something like absolute reasons, and therefore something like GE1, in mind when formulating his argument, and that the possibility of absolute reasons coming apart from rationalizing reasons in God's case was not live in his thinking. For this reason, I will offer my responses on the assumption that the proponent of Rowe's argument is thinking in terms of GE1.[7]

If we understand gratuitousness in terms of GE1, then we can now see a quite general reason why we might be suspicious about the theological premise.[8] Suppose that at the time of the occurrence of e, God reasonably acted on the supposition that permitting it would have no net moral cost, but as a matter of contingent fact it has turned out that the moral costs of the permission ended up outweighing the moral costs that would have been incurred by prevention. Or suppose that at the time of the occurrence of e, God reasonably acted on the supposition that preventing it would have no net moral cost, but as a matter of contingent fact it has turned out that the moral costs of the prevention ended up outweighing the moral costs that would have been incurred by permission. In cases like these, the existence of some gratuitous evils is compatible with the existence of God. This is because the occurrence of these evils may be due to a form of ignorance on God's part that remains, in a way I will try to articulate, in keeping with divine omniscience. In such cases God has a rationalizing reason for allowing the evils to occur even though it turns out that there is no absolute reason for doing so. If there can be cases like these, then it seems that the theological premise is not a pure conceptual necessity.

So, how could God's ignorance regarding the gratuitousness of some cases of serious suffering be compatible with divine omniscience? Well, without going too theologically far afield, we can answer very briefly by just sketching the position that has come to be known as Open Theism.[9] According to Open Theism, though God knows everything that can possibly be known (and that's what makes God omniscient), there are some things that not even an omniscient being can know. In particular, Open Theists typically emphasize the unknowability of those future events that genuinely depend on the robust free will of human beings. The aspects of the future that depend on the exercise of free will are not merely unknown by God (or anyone else) but are *unknowable*. This is why God's failure to know them does not count against divine omniscience. Knowledge of the content and consequences of future free choices is, then, analogous to the ability to perform actions that constitute logical contradictions. Both are incoherent; just as it is no strike against divine omnipotence that God cannot make a round square, so it is no strike against divine omniscience that God cannot know what someone will freely choose in the future.

To fill in some details that might, on the assumption of Open Theism, make the case for the possible falsity of TP more forceful, imagine that God must decide whether or not to permit, say, an instance of leukemia. Imagine further that, given God's knowledge, it is reasonable for God to act on the supposition that the sufferer and his family will respond to the leukemia with strength and hope. In fact, however, after the diagnosis they use their freedom to turn against each other, to abandon faith and the common bonds of support, and decline into depressive isolation from each other and God.[10] In this case, it may be that the suffering would not have been gratuitous if the sufferers had used their free will in the ways that God reasonably supposed they would. However, in using their free will as they did (and contrary to God's reasonable supposition about how they would use it), the suffering that actually occurs involves a net moral loss. In a case like this, it can turn out that God had a rationalizing reason to permit the leukemia but no absolute reason to do so.[11] What this shows, I believe, is that at least some theists – those, for example, who are inclined toward an Open view – can have good grounds for refusing to accept Rowe's theological premise.[12]

Nevertheless, it remains a reasonable and open (pardon the pun) question whether the costs of accepting Open Theism, both for the problem of evil and elsewhere, are worth the local gain here of giving the theist a sensible reason to resist TP.[13]

3.5   The Moorean Shift

Even in the original presentation of his evidential argument from evil, Rowe (1979) was sensitive to a possible line of response that would represent only an indirect challenge to his empirical premise (that there are some gratuitous evils). What he noted was that an argumentative maneuver roughly parallel to G. E. Moore's famous response to external world skepticism is available to the theist. In short, the theist might be able to take advantage of the fact that one person's *modus ponens* is another person's *modus tollens*. Here's what I mean.

Moore took himself to be confronting an argument like this:

1. I do not know that I am not a brain in a vat.
2. If I do not know that I am not a brain in a vat, then I do not know I have hands.
3. Therefore, I do not know I have hands (and if we generalize from this conclusion, we get global skepticism about the world outside our minds).

But rather than challenging either of the first two premises directly, we can think of Moore as developing a parallel argument that he took to be at least as strong as this skeptical one.

1*. I know I have hands.
 2. If I do not know that I am not a brain in a vat, then I do not know I have hands.

3*. Therefore, I know I'm not a brain in a vat (and, more generally, I don't have to worry about global skepticism).

Notice that the second premise has stayed the same. The first premise in this argument is just the denial of the conclusion of the original skeptical argument. And this gives us the denial of the first premise of the original skeptical argument as our new conclusion. How forceful you take this strategy to be will depend on how you assess the initial comparative plausibility of premise 1 and premise 1*. Are you more confident that you have hands or that you don't know you are not a brain in a vat? Obviously, Moore thinks you should be more confident that you have hands – and skepticism is thusly refuted (or something near enough).

Rowe notes, then, that the theist can approach the evidential argument from evil in a similar way. The parallel "Moorean Shift" argument will be something like:

1*. God exists.
 2. If God exists, then there are no gratuitous evils.
3*. Therefore, there are no gratuitous evils.

Again, premise 1* is the denial of Rowe's original conclusion; premise 2 has stayed the same (this is just our elliptical version of the Theological Premise); and the new conclusion (3*) is the denial of Rowe's first premise. How forceful you take this strategy to be will depend on how you assess the initial comparative plausibility of premise 1 from Rowe's argument and premise 1* from the Moorean Shift argument. Are you more confident that there are gratuitous evils or that God exists?

Now, one way to make the Moorean Shift response to Rowe's argument particularly powerful would be to offer some very good independent reasons for thinking that God does exist. In fact, if the independent arguments for the existence of God are strong enough, they could (at least in principle) render Rowe's argument a complete failure. There are a couple of things to say about this possibility, though. The first is that however the final assessment of the traditional arguments for God's existence ultimately stands, the soundness of these arguments has not been so widely and deeply accepted as to constitute or contribute much to a *general* refutation of the evidential argument from evil. The second thing to note is that in order for an argument for God's existence to support the Moorean Shift response to Rowe's argument, it will have to support the claim that an *omnibenevolent* being exists. That is, since premise 1* of the Moorean Shift argument has to involve the existence of the kind of being that would not permit gratuitous evils (as the second premise insists), any argument in its support will have to show *more* than that some maximally powerful and knowledgeable being exists (Trakakis 2005). The trouble here is that many (maybe even most) of the traditional arguments for God's existence – the various versions of the cosmological and teleological arguments, for example – simply can't reasonably be taken to support the claim, by themselves, that a maximally good being exists. From these arguments, even if they are sound, the best we get is that the universe has an all-powerful and all-knowing creator and/or sustainer. By contrast, versions of the ontological argument (and perhaps of the moral argument) at least purport to produce the conclusion that an omnibenevolent being exists (cf. Byrne 2007; Oppy 2011). If the theist hopes to execute the Moorean Shift by way of arguing for premise 1*, then she will have to deploy such arguments (Tooley 2012).

But must a proponent of the Moorean Shift response to Rowe's evidential argument support premise 1* by appealing to independent evidence for the existence of God? Not obviously. On a plausible and influential view (namely, Alvin Plantinga's), belief in God – that is, in a perfectly powerful, knowledgeable, and loving creator of the universe – can be warranted even in the absence of positive evidence for the existence of God in the form of arguments or experiences (Plantinga 2000). If this is right, then it is at least possible that some theists have enough warrant, even in the absence of positive evidence, for their acceptance of premise 1* that it constitutes good grounds for accepting 3* – that there are no gratuitous evils.

We should admit, however, that the dialectical situation here is delicate. It would be at least flat-footed, and more likely intellectually dishonest, for the theist simply to insist that her belief in the existence of God is insulated from counterevidence by virtue of its arising in a properly basic way. This is because beliefs that get their warrant non-inferentially must still be able to face defeaters. To illustrate, suppose it is true that sense experience is a basic source of warrant for our beliefs. And further suppose that your belief that a red ball is in front of you is arising from sense experience. It doesn't follow directly from these two suppositions that you are warranted in believing that the ball in front of you is red. After all, you may have some powerful defeater for this belief. For example, suppose you also know that this room is regularly radiated by a red light that makes white objects appear red. In this case, even though sense experience is a basic source of warrant for you, the presence of a defeater for the belief arising from sense experience seems to block or undercut the transfer of warrant from the basic source to your belief. We can see now, I hope, that even if belief in God can be properly basic in a way parallel to your red-ball belief, it isn't a straightforward matter to deploy premise 1* in an argument to the conclusion that there are no gratuitous evils. This is because Rowe's appeal to the supposed existence of gratuitous evils (like E1 and E2) can be taken as an effort to show that the theist has a defeater for her theistic belief even if this belief does happen to have arisen in the basic way.

The thing to conclude from this, however, does not seem to me to be that the Moorean Shift strategy can only be executed by offering independent evidence for premise 1*. For there are defeaters and then there are defeaters. Notice that I framed the red radiation defeater above in terms of your knowing that the room is *regularly* radiated with red light. But suppose, instead, that the purported defeater is only that, for all you know, the room *has sometimes* been radiated by red light. Now it is not at all clear that you have a defeater strong enough to undo the basic warrant, by way of sense experience, that you have for your belief that the ball in front of you is red. With respect to this kind of response to Rowe's argument, then, the question is whether the theist's assessment of the claim that there are gratuitous evils puts her more in your epistemic position with respect to the red ball when you know that the room is regularly radiated with red light, or more in your epistemic position with respect to the red ball when you know only that the room has sometimes been so radiated. I suspect that the assessment is going to vary from theist to theist. Thus, whether a Moorean approach without independent evidence can succeed will also vary.

3.6   Going Deeper: The Skepticism in Skeptical Theism

We have now seen a few potential theistic responses to Rowe's evidential argument from evil. On my view, each of those I have canvassed (the appeal to Skeptical Theism, the appeal to Open Theism, and the appeal to the Moorean Shift) have merit and could, under certain conditions, constitute a forceful defense of the rationality of theistic belief in the face of the existence of putatively gratuitous evil. It is probably clear, however, that I take the response of skeptical theism to be the most generally promising. Not only is it the response most widely available to theists of many different stripes, depending, as it does, on commitments reasonably shared by almost every version of common theism, but I believe it also gives expression to a naturally desirable and intuitively reasonable form of intellectual humility. I am convinced that the propriety of this species of intellectual humility can be justified, regardless of whether one is inclined toward theism. It would be quite reasonable even for the atheist to be skeptical about the truth of (GOODS). However, Skeptical Theism has received substantial criticism. Probably the most penetrating form has attempted to demonstrate that the skepticism in Skeptical Theism cannot be kept in its place. Various critics have argued, in other words, that embracing Skeptical Theism will force us into a more general and unacceptable form of skepticism, perhaps epistemological or perhaps moral (cf. Gale 1996; Russell 1996; Almeida and Oppy 2003; Wilks 2009). In essence, then, these critics of Skeptical Theism believe that they can reduce the view to absurdity by showing that it leads to conflicts with our ordinary epistemic and moral practices.

The crucial question, then, is whether anyone who is skeptical about the truth of (GOODS) – that is, anyone who takes it to be reasonable to withhold judgment with respect to the claim that we would probably be able to recognize the considerations that justify God in permitting the evils we find if such considerations existed – must also be skeptical more generally. Remember that the skeptical theist need not insist that (GOODS) is false; it is enough, on my reconstruction of the skeptical theist's strategy, that it be reasonable to withhold judgment regarding the truth of Rowe's empirical premise. Since the support for this premise is a noseeum argument that depends on the truth of (GOODS), a defense in response to this argument can rest with a case that the probability that we would be able to recognize God's justifying reasons is not high. Thus, (GOODS) can be resisted if the probability that we would be able to recognize God's justifying reasons is either *inscrutable* or *low*. This means that the too-much-skepticism complaint depends on showing us that accepting the low or inscrutable probability that we would be able to recognize God's justifying reasons for permitting the world's horrors will entail the wider forms of skepticism that we all hope to avoid.

To make the case as favorable to the critics of skeptical theism as possible, let's assume a version of skeptical theism making the strongest epistemic claim: namely, that (GOODS) is *false* because the probability in question is actually *low*. How are we supposed to get from this claim to the wilder and woolier skepticisms? Perhaps like this. If we become convinced that we are unlikely to recognize God's reasons for permitting evils like E1 and E2, then for all we know God has reasons unrecognizable to us for doing or permitting all sorts of things we can't rule out. God could have reasons, then, for creating the world ten minutes ago so as to look billions of years old. God could have reasons for permitting an evil demon to deceive us into thinking we have hands when we are actually just brains in vats. Since it is generally unlikely that we would be able to recognize the reasons that God would have for doing or permitting these things, we are stuck with them as serious epistemic possibilities, and the broad skeptical conclusion would seem to follow forthwith.

The problem with this line of reasoning is that the skeptical theist is not pressed by her rejection of (GOODS) into any unique commitment to the seriousness of the epistemic possibilities countenanced above. No doubt it is true that God could have reasons for creating or permitting the pernicious epistemic situations I have described. But this is just the general problem of external world skepticism that *everyone* faces. There is no special problem for the skeptical theist here. The appearance of a special problem may be generated by the mistaken extrapolation from the claim that we are unlikely to recognize God's reasons for permitting the world's evils to the claim that we are unlikely to recognize *any* of God's reasons whatsoever. It is important to see that the skeptical theist need not accept anything nearly so general as skepticism about all of God's reasons. Indeed, it is fully compatible with skeptical theism that we have been given a great deal of knowledge about God's reasoning either by the light of natural reason or by revelation or both. This means that there is nothing to block the skeptical theist from deploying whatever anti-skepticism strategy you happen to favor in response to the general problem of external world skepticism, and this while continuing to maintain that we probably wouldn't be able to recognize the considerations that justify God in permitting the world's evils. Put another way, the too-much-skepticism complaint turns on the thought that being skeptical about (GOODS) is about as unreasonable as being skeptical about our being brains-in-vats or our living in a ten-minute-old world. But surely the epistemic humility that would lead one to think that we probably wouldn't recognize the reasons that an Anselmian being would have for allowing particular evils is not as unreasonable as the attitude toward epistemic possibilities exemplified by the radical skeptic.[14]

A more forceful version of the too-much-skepticism complaint, however, can be framed by constraining the worry to the moral domain (cf. Russell 1996; Almeida and Oppy 2003). The concern, then, is not that rejecting (GOODS) leads to an unacceptable general skepticism, but rather that it leads to an unacceptable moral skepticism. Suppose you were in position to save the deer from the forest fire in E1 or to stop the brutality in E2. It seems clear that you ought to do so. That is, it seems clear that you *know* that it would be morally right, even morally obligatory, for you to intervene. According to these moral critics of skeptical theism, though, if you reject (GOODS), then it isn't so clear after all. If the reasons God may have for permitting E1 and E2 are probably beyond your ken, then even though you can't see what reason there might be to do nothing, there may be such reasons. What seems morally obvious – that you ought to intervene – turns out to be morally ambiguous on the assumption of skeptical theism, and this is a profound strike against skeptical theism.

Again, though, we need to ask if this moral ambiguity really does follow from rejecting (GOODS). We can begin to see a problem by noting how deaf we would be to anyone who attempted to justify her failure to intervene in a situation like E1 or E2 by appealing to the fact that *God* must have had good reasons for allowing these horrible events. Our deafness will be the result, I suggest, of our commitment to the idea that the moral demands on us are a product of the reasons *we have*, where both the "we" and the "have" are important.

If you are the subject of a moral demand to do something, then it is the set of reasons *you* have to do the thing that matters – not the set of reasons that I (or God) may have for doing the thing. When I was about four years old, my dad came into a room to find me faux-smoking a cigarette I'd found lying around. His strategy (one I am mostly inclined to endorse) was to offer to light it up for me. When he did, you can guess what happened. After the hacking and horror of the experience, I have never taken the idea of smoking seriously. Whatever you are inclined to think of this approach yourself, you will surely allow that while it might have been acceptable for my dad to execute it, it would not have been acceptable for a random stranger at the park to do so. The stranger at the park just bears the wrong relationship to me to be taking up this approach; she doesn't have the *right* to do this, even if she really cares that I don't become a smoker. Thus, from the fact that my father may have had a justifying reason to light me up, it does not follow that someone else has this same justifying reason. Similarly, from the fact that God may have a justifying reason to permit some horrible event, it simply does not follow that anyone else has this same justifying reason.

In addition, if you are the subject of a moral demand to do something, then it is the set of reasons you *have* to do the thing that matters – not the set of reasons *there may be* for doing the thing. Now, what it is for a person to *have* a reason rather than there merely *being* one is a subject of substantive controversy. Still, there is clearly a difference, and at least minimally, it has something to do with the epistemic access the agent has to the reasons there are. An agent's having a reason to do something must involve at least the agent's being able to recognize the considerations in favor of doing the thing. Suppose I believe that you are going to die of thirst if I don't get you some water quickly, and suppose I also believe that this clear substance is water. Then I have a moral reason to give you this substance. If the substance is actually a poison and I neither know nor should know this fact, then there is an important sense in which I still do not have a reason to withhold the substance from you. I retain the justifying reason to give you the substance despite the fact that there *is* a reason *not* to give it to you: namely, that it will kill you. Similarly, given that God's reasons for permitting E1 and E2 are, by hypothesis, not accessible to us, they can't be *our* reasons. We can't *have* those reasons, even if there *are* such reasons. I am inclined to conclude then that skepticism about (GOODS) does not entail skepticism about all of morality or lead to untoward consequences for our moral deliberation.[15] For this reason, the defensive strategy deployed by skeptical theists seems to me to be substantially, even if provisionally, successful.

3.7 Conclusion

William Rowe's development of the evidential argument for atheism is powerful and incisive. It is, in fact, a remarkably valuable model of philosophy of religion done right in every relevant respect – analytically precise, intellectually fair, and existentially sensitive.[16] Nevertheless, I have tried to show that equally precise, fair, and sensitive responses can be mustered that preserve the basic rationality of theistic commitment. None of this is to say, however, that evidential arguments from evil are unsuccessful *simpliciter*. Though I conclude that theism remains rational in the face of evidential arguments, it might nevertheless be rational for atheists to find support for their atheism in them as well. I have made no effort here to argue to the contrary. And what of the as-yet uncommitted inquirer into the existence of God? What should such a person think about the probity of the evidential arguments with respect to her inquiry? Here I am content to leave this as an open question for further consideration.

Finally, and by way of transition to the next chapter, we should return to one of the crucial analogies to which opponents of Rowe's evidential argument have regularly appealed – the parent analogy. According to the skeptical theistic response to the evidential argument, God's relation to us with respect to the existence of horrendous suffering may be like the parent's relation to her child with respect to chemotherapy. For all we know, that is, there are good reasons for the permission of the suffering but, like the young child with cancer, none of us is in a position to recognize, understand, or appreciate these reasons. In response to this analogy, Rowe makes a very powerful point. In essence, he argues that this analogy actually cuts against the case for theism. This is because a good parent, in anything like the chemotherapy situation, will deal with her child's incapacity to apprehend the reasons for the treatment by making very special efforts to be close to her child, to comfort and assure her child that there *is* a good reason for the suffering, and to communicate that the child is not alone in it. "So," Rowe says, "on the basis of the good-parent analogy, we should infer that it is likely that God too will almost always be consciously present to humans, if not other animals, when he permits them to suffer for goods they cannot comprehend, giving special assurances of his love for them" (2001, 131). Unfortunately, as Rowe notes, it certainly seems like there are vast numbers of people who endure gruesome hardships with no special word or comfort from God. Accordingly, the analogy actually supports the thesis that God does not exist.

I grant, again, that this is indeed an important challenge. Notice, however, that the atheistic conclusion would seem to follow only on the assumption (perhaps among others) that we are not justified in thinking that God has good reasons for remaining silent under such conditions. Are we unjustified in thinking that God has such reasons? This question will bring us to the central issue of the next chapter. The silence (or "hiddenness") of God – both in general and in the special circumstances to which Rowe draws our attention – can reasonably be taken to be a particular species of putative evil that can be put to work in a further argument against the existence of God. Thus even if, as I have suggested, the rationality of theistic belief is not essentially undermined by the evidential argument, the "problem of divine hiddenness" puts novel pressure on it.

4

The Problem of Divine Hiddenness

Almost everyone wants for a bit more confidence that the God of common theism exists.[1] Matters in this domain could certainly be clearer. If you are anything like me (and I'm certainly not wishing this on you), you will be able to recall a few episodes in your childhood, or perhaps even later, of hoping for, or even seeking, some decisive confirmation of the existence of God. More than once I asked God simply to flip my bedroom light off and quickly back on; that's all I thought I needed. I won't keep you in suspense about the outcome. Nothing happened. I am willing to bet that the same has been true for you in any analogous efforts.

As thoughtful adults now (let's suppose), we can probably dismiss the negative results of these immature explorations as having very little probative value. Still, the fact that existence of God is not more obvious than it in fact is does suggest a problem. The most pointed version of this problem, the one that will be the focus of our attention in this chapter, has come – rather infelicitously, I think – to be known as the Problem of Divine Hiddenness. Part of the problem with this terminology is that a number of distinct problems seem to run under this banner and keeping them sorted out can be confusing. For example, there does appear to be a quite general explanatory problem for theism with respect to the fact that God's existence is not more transparent. That is, as Blaise Pascal regularly recognizes throughout his *Pensées*, the theist ought to have something to say about why God operates in such a way that the terminology of *deus absconditus* is so clearly appropriate. Notice, though, that the existence of this explanatory problem of hiddenness need not be thought to generate any special challenge for the justification of theistic belief. This is because the explanatory problem could remain even if every single human being were given enough evidence to make it rational for him or her to accept theism. Supposing all of us to have sufficient warrant for theistic commitments, we could still wonder together why the existence of God has not been made more manifest – why we are not able to be aware of God the way, for example, we are able to be aware of our immediate physical surroundings or our own personal existence. So this explanatory hiddenness problem is not our topic, since we are worried about those contemporary problems of purported evil that constitute rational objections to theistic belief.

The intuitive idea behind the problem that *will* be our topic in this chapter can helpfully be explicated by thinking of the hiddenness of God as the existence of *reasonable non-belief*. God is hidden in the sense that there are some people who, despite having both the rational capacities and volitional dispositions to believe that God exists, find themselves without the experiences or evidences they reasonably require in order to manifest this belief. They have been open-minded and thoughtful about the possibility that God exists but simply cannot draw the theistic conclusion, given the evidence available to them. On this view, God is not necessarily hidden from *everyone*. Many people do believe that God exists, and many of these people may have evidence sufficient to justify their belief. Still, according to what we will call "the polemical problem of divine hiddenness," God is hidden from some people, and this is enough to provide the grounds for a powerful argument against the existence of God. This is because, if God exists, proponents of this argument insist, then God would not be hidden from *anyone* – there would be *no* people who inculpably fail to believe that God exists.

Now you may be asking why we are treating this polemical problem of hiddenness in a book on the problems of evil. There is a clear disciplinary answer that remains somewhat conceptually controversial. The clear disciplinary answer is that contemporary philosophers of religion have generally taken these problems to bear an intellectual family resemblance to each other. One popular way of taking notice of the resemblance is by thinking of divine hiddenness as a particular kind or instance of evil and of the polemical argument itself as parallel to one or another of the arguments from evil at which we have already looked. In fact, I suggested this way of thinking about the hiddenness problem when initially presenting it in chapter 1. However, this is precisely where the potential controversy emerges. Some philosophers do indeed claim that the polemical problem of hiddenness just is, or is a species of, the traditional problem of evil; others insist that it presents a unique problem for theistic belief that would have to be faced even if there were no problem of evil as such (cf. Kvanvig 2001 and van Inwagen 2001, respectively). I will leave for homework the project of determining who is right here. Whoever you end up siding with, it still makes sense to reflect on the hiddenness argument for atheism in the context of the problem of evil. As we will see, the structures of the arguments and the theistic strategies of response are so clearly analogous and so frequently overlapping that the family resemblance justification for treating the hiddenness problem together with the problem of evil is compelling. Furthermore, as we saw with Rowe's response to the parent analogy at the end of chapter 3, our confrontations with evil seem at least to bring the problem of hiddenness quite crisply into view and raise the stakes for a solution.[2]

The most influential contemporary presentation of the polemical problem of divine hiddenness is that of J. L. Schellenberg. In 1993, he published his monograph *Divine Hiddenness and Human Reason*, which can now be considered the headwaters of a substantial river of new work on the implications of the existence of unbelief for the rationality of theistic commitment. We will have space in this chapter to explore only the main features of Schellenberg's argument, and survey, from some metaphorical height above, the path of its philosophical effluence.

4.1   The Polemical Problem of Divine Hiddenness: Schellenberg's Argument

Schellenberg's argument is marked by a couple of fresh emphases. First, he emphasizes what he takes to be an essential feature of God, if such a being exists: namely, that such a being is essentially loving. Perhaps it is an obvious corollary of God's omnibenevolence or maximal goodness that God is perfectly loving. But perhaps not. A being could be perfectly good – say, perfectly fair and just – without having the sort of concern for creatures that is characteristic of love. In any case, Schellenberg insists, in essence, that even if there exists a being who has created the universe and is omnipotent and omniscient but who is also in any way less than perfectly loving, then this being does not get to count as God.

Furthermore, Schellenberg sensitively draws out an insight about unbelief from considerations about perfect love. If a perfectly loving God exists, then having a certain kind of relationship with this being is bound to be central to human flourishing. Specifically, Schellenberg emphasizes the value to each human life of enjoying a reciprocal relationship of mutual and communicative intimacy with such a being. This kind of intimate relationship with the loving creator of the universe would be both intrinsically good and a fundamental source of moral good for the creature, providing moral strength, restorative forgiveness, and unlimited hope in the face of any personal or social failings. Given the great good to each human life of such a relationship, a loving God would seek such relationship with every creature capable of it. But, Schellenberg claims, for a creature to have a reciprocal relationship with God, the creature must believe that God exists. It is possible, of course, that some creatures, created with robust freedom, will not want to be related to God in this reciprocal way and therefore that some of them will use the freedom of their wills to avoid believing in God by ignoring evidence, hardening their hearts against God's communications, and the like. However, given perfect divine love, God would make sure that every creature who is *willing* to be in life-giving reciprocal relationship with her creator is also *able* to be. And, since belief in the existence of God is necessary for enjoying this kind of relationship, God would make sure that every creature who is willing to be in such a relationship is *able to believe* in God's existence. What we should conclude from these reflections on perfect love, relationship, and belief, according to Schellenberg, is that if God exists, then no one who is willing to be in relationship with God will also be unable to believe that God exists.

Finally, Schellenberg emphasizes that there certainly appear to be people who, though they would be happy to be in relationship with God, find themselves unable to believe that God exists. Some fair-minded and relationally sensitive people you know may already be leaping immediately to mind – people whose responsible assessment of the evidence for God's existence has left them quite honestly (and often quite distressingly) in a state of agnosticism on the question. It is no surprise that the community of contemporary philosophers of religion is populated by a number of these individuals. I won't name those whom I myself take to be the most excellent cases in point. It will have to suffice to say that I am frequently impressed, both in what I read and in what I see in interpersonal relationships, with what for all the world appears to me to be the intellectual integrity and volitional tenderness of numerous colleagues who seem forced to conclude that the evidence for theism is just too thin for them. If Schellenberg is right (and you can see my own temptation to agree with him on this point), then there is *reasonable* (or sometimes he refers to it as *inculpable*) unbelief; there are people who are unable to believe that God exists and their inability is not due to some blameworthy cognitive or volitional effort or dysfunction on their own part. However, we saw above that it is just this kind of unbelief (the unbelief of fair and honest inquirers without an axe to grind against God or religious belief) that a loving God would not permit – and precisely because permitting it would involve blocking the possibility of a loving reciprocal relationship of essential importance for human good. Therefore, the existence of this form of unbelief provides us with strong grounds for concluding that no perfectly loving being exists.

Going forward, it will be useful to have Schellenberg's regimentation of this argument before us. He presents it this way:

(1) If there is a God, he is perfectly loving.
(2) If a perfectly loving God exists, reasonable nonbelief does not occur.
(3) Reasonable nonbelief occurs.
(4) Therefore, no perfectly loving God exists [from (2) and (3)].
(5) Therefore, there is no God [from (1) and (4)]. (1993, 83)[3]

We should also keep in mind that Schellenberg conceives of this argument in predominantly evidential terms. Thus, we should be thinking of his argument roughly as we also thought of Rowe's argument from apparently gratuitous evils; the atheistic conclusion is *made probable* by the premises and by the kind of support the premises have received. Once again, then, this argument does not, like Mackie's, purport to uncover a fundamental logical inconsistency in the necessary commitments of theism. Rather, and somewhat more precisely, though Schellenberg may think that (1) is a conceptual truth, his initial defense of the crucial premises [(2) and (3)] attempts to show that they are plausibly true, on strictly evidential grounds.[4] The conclusion, then, must be taken as having only the evidential strength of the premises.[5]

4.2   Challenging the Reasonable Nonbelief Premise

The first premise of Schellenberg's argument, linking God with perfect love, has gone essentially unchallenged. Premises (2) and (3), however, have been subject to considerable critical attention. In this section we will take up the efforts to resist (3) – according to which there are, in fact, people who are unable to believe that God exists despite being both willing and able to respond well to the evidence for God's existence. Before doing so, however, let's remind ourselves of the main reasons for thinking that (3) is true. In short, these are reasons derived from our experience with what seem to us to be reasonable nonbelievers. Specifically, we have encountered individuals who have concluded, on the basis of responsible investigation, that there are no compelling considerations favoring the claim that God exists over the claim that God does not exist. For a defense in response to Schellenberg's polemical problem of hiddenness to succeed here, the defender will need to show us how the theist could plausibly reject (3). A couple of strategies for showing this have been tried.

The first strategy has been to draw on the influential tradition of attributing unbelief to sinfulness. If all nonbelief is, at some level of abstraction, reasonably thought to be due to human moral failing, then premise (3) can plausibly be rejected. And one important source of this influential tradition appears to be the Christian scripture itself. The apostle Paul famously insists, in his epistle to the Romans, that:

> [t]he wrath of God is being revealed from heaven against all godlessness and wickedness of people, who suppress the truth by their wickedness, since what may be known about God is plain to them. For since the creation of the world God's invisible qualities – his eternal power and divine nature – have been clearly seen, being understood from what has been made, so that people are without excuse. (Romans 1:18–20 NIV)

The Pauline picture, then, seems to be one according to which the unbelief of those he has in mind is due principally to some form of willful resistance to the clear truth about the existence of God, an effort to "suppress" the truth that is otherwise quite clear. If Paul's account can be taken as a plausible diagnosis of all theistic nonbelief, then indeed premise (3) could, on these grounds, be rejected.[6]

But would this be a plausible diagnosis? Not obviously – and not even from the standpoint of the committed theist. Of course it is almost certainly true that there are nonbelievers who are inclined to resist evidence for theism in just the way that Paul describes. Attempting to account for *all* unbelief in these terms, however, is not particularly charitable or sensible. Again, we must confront the original evidence to which Schellenberg and others appeal: namely, the existence of apparently responsible nonbelievers. Simply to insist that all of these apparently responsible nonbelievers are really just suppressing the truth would not be to address the purported evidence so much as it would seem to involve denying that it exists. Part of what makes the denial of the existence of this evidence awkward, even for the committed theist, is that

many of those who have become believers were once nonbelievers – nonbelievers that, as their present belief indicates,
were willing to believe on strong enough evidence or experi-
ential support. Now, some extant believers will think back
about their earlier unbelieving selves as people who were
downright resisting belief. But not all will. Many will describe
themselves as having been open to evidences and experiences
they simply had not yet received. Resisting premise (3) by
appeal to a generalization from the Pauline description does
not, then, appear to be a promising tack.

A more subtle appeal to human sinfulness in efforts to
resist (3) can be found in an emphasis on the "noetic effects
of sin" (cf. Murray 1993; Plantinga 2000; Wainwright 2001).
Just as the misuse of our free will can result in damage to our
volitional faculties, so can it result in damage to our intellectual faculties. Here the claim is not that the nonbeliever is
sinfully suppressing the truth, but rather that the nonbeliever's sinfulness (or perhaps the more general sinfulness of
humanity) infects or contributes to the diminishment of her
cognitive capacities in such a way that unbelief seems, contrary to fact, reasonable. If this sinfulness were removed,
claims this objector to premise (3), God's existence would be
sufficiently clear. Since our sinfulness is something for which
we are responsible, the nonbelief that results from it is also
our responsibility, and no fault of God's. There is, then, no
reasonable (i.e. inculpable) nonbelief.

Theistic traditions that have emphasized human "fallen-
ness" and the impact of moral corruption on cognitive incapacity may be able to get some leverage out of this sort of
response to premise (3). But the case is not an easy one to
make. Even if there can be seen to be some plausibility to the
idea that the intellect can be damaged by sin, insisting that
all apparently reasonable unbelief is due to sin can succeed
as a defense in response to Schellenberg's argument only if
the following can also be shown to be plausible from the
point of view of the theist: either (1) that each person's unbelief is causally related to her own sin or (2) that we can be
properly held responsible for the sin of others – by virtue of
being held responsible for the cognitive incapacities with
which human sin in general has left each of us. The path to
neither is particularly promising.

4.3   Challenging the Conditional Premise

We have seen already the broad reasons mustered in support of the conditional second premise. At root, the central considerations in favor of premise (2) involve the connection between belief and the deep goodness of reciprocal relationship with God. Since belief that God exists is necessary for the form of intimacy between God and human beings that Schellenberg emphasizes, a perfectly loving creator would insure that only the unreasonably or immorally resistant are incapable of this belief. Thus, if such a being exists, there would be no reasonable unbelief.

A successful defensive response to this aspect of the polemical problem of hiddenness would have to show that it is plausible for the theist at least to withhold judgment about the truth of premise (2). We would, therefore, have to be able to imagine circumstances in which the antecedent of the conditional is true (a perfectly loving God exists) and also in which, for all the theist knows, the consequent is false (there *is* some reasonable nonbelief). Theistic efforts to present such cases can be categorized into two broad groups: *securing goods* defenses and *avoiding evils* defenses.

In the spirit of securing goods, a number of critics of Schellenberg's argument have urged us to see that there may be some great goods that God could bring about only by permitting some reasonable unbelief. What goods, then, might the permission of reasonable unbelief be thought to help secure? Here are a few potentially interrelated suggestions. First, it might be a great good for human beings not simply to come to believe that God exists but to do so as a result of *seeking*, as a result of real cognitive and volitional effort. Such seeking demands that there be some period of time during which the seeker is a reasonable unbeliever.[7] Second, it might be a great good for human beings to have a kind of relationship with God that is not the result of an imposed presence of God. Perhaps a special sort of love and trust is possible between a human being and God only if the human being enters into it in the absence of sufficient evidence. Third, it might be a great good for human beings to choose to act well *freely* rather than as the result of a kind of divine coercion. However, some have argued that it would, in effect, be coercive for God to act in the way demanded by proponents of Schellenberg's argument (cf. Murray 1993, 2001; Swinburne 2004). To be provided with evidence strong enough to make reasonable unbelief impossible would be, at least for some, to be unable to resist acting rightly and doing good – perhaps out of fear of eternal damnation or because of the transparent goodness of the eternal life promised by God. Thus, strong enough evidence for the existence of God would coerce (some) people into acting as God would want them to act. That is, removing all reasonable unbelief would undermine the possibility of an important good: namely, the good of human beings *freely* choosing to act well.

Unfortunately for the theist, the suggestion that any of these three goods might justify God in allowing reasonable nonbelief faces a debilitating objection. For there appear to be instances wherein the goods under consideration are either comparatively unimportant or secured despite the fact that reasonable nonbelief has been eliminated. Cases of this sort will be any of those in which a person has come to a particularly firm belief in the existence of God – perhaps, but not necessarily, as the result of a profound religious experience. As a case in point, consider the Apostle Paul who, according to the New Testament, came to believe in the Christian God as a result of being blinded, knocked off a horse, and receiving a very specific (apparently verbal) message from God. Theists (particularly of the Christian variety) will generally have to grant that Paul had a deep personal relationship with God – it is, after all, presented to Christians as a paradigm. It would also be implausible to insist that Paul's firm belief in God's existence coerced him in such a way as to make his genuine moral progress problematic. And even if Paul did not have the "opportunity" to seek God in the way the first version of this objection to premise (2) emphasizes, it is hard to see the great good that Paul thereby lost out on. In any case, it would not appear to have been a good so valuable that the God of the Christian scriptures was unwilling to sacrifice it in this situation. Furthermore, I have selected Paul as an especially iconic illustration of the more general point. Surely there are many more mundane examples of people who seem to enjoy a firm confidence in the existence of God but who do not seem to have lost out on important goods, either of relationship with God or of moral development, as a result.[8]

Perhaps a stronger case for resisting premise (2) can be made by appealing to evils God would hope to avoid rather than to goods God would seek to secure. Are there any evils that the theist could reasonably believe God could avoid only by permitting inculpable nonbelief? Here is a suggestion. Suppose what God wants for human beings is to enter into a deep and reciprocal relationship, like the one Schellenberg emphasizes, with each one of them. Suppose further, and plausibly, that there is considerably more to entering into this kind of relationship than simply believing that God exists. So, though belief is necessary for this relationship, a great deal more is required of human beings: trust, submission, obedience, and the like of these, for example. It is possible (indeed, probable), however, that there are people who would not go on to meet these further requirements even after coming to believe in the existence of God. That is, there are almost certainly some *poor responders* to good evidence for God's existence – people who would nevertheless refuse to trust, submit to, and obey God. Now, some of these poor responders may be such that they would never enter into the relevant kind of intimate relationship with God, no matter at what point in their lives they came to believe in God's existence. For such people, it isn't at all clear that God's failure to grant them evidence sufficient for their belief is any sort of harm to them, since this belief will never lead on to the important relationship. In fact, God's granting them belief under these conditions may be an evil – since it may be a substantial evil to refuse to enter into the intimate relationship with God after coming to believe in God's existence. Thus, if God fails to grant sufficient evidence to such people, then they are kept from this evil. Furthermore, it may be that some poor responders will only respond poorly to their belief in the existence of God if the belief comes about at or before a certain time or under certain conditions. These people might respond well, though, if their belief in the existence of God arises later, for example. For such people, God avoids a very serious evil – the evil of these people refusing to enter into the right relationship with God despite having the necessary belief – by permitting their reasonable nonbelief at the present time.

Though there is some force in this reply, giving the theist some grounds for resisting premise (2), we should wonder if it can do enough. The reason to doubt that it can is that it offers an account of the existence of reasonable nonbelief only for *poor responders* – only, that is, for people who would not take the opportunity afforded by belief in the existence of God to go on to enter into an intimate and reciprocal relationship with God.[9] How plausible is the idea that only poor responders are the subjects of reasonable nonbelief? Not very. This means that the polemical problem of hiddenness could simply be reframed around the existence of reasonable nonbelievers who are *not* poor responders. The theist who hopes to offer a defense along these lines in response to Schellenberg's argument will now need either to make it plausible to suppose that all reasonable nonbelief occurs only in poor responders or to extend her defense to account for the reasonable nonbelief of some good responders. I conclude, then, that the *avoiding evils* response to premise (2) needs fuller development and is therefore of limited value.[10,11]

4.4   Skeptical Theism Once Again

Recall, however, that in the last chapter I assessed the skeptical theistic defense in response to Rowe's evidential argument as a provisional success. I concluded that it is quite sensible for the theist (and, indeed, for the atheist as well) to be skeptical about the truth of (GOODS), according to which human beings like us would probably be able to figure out what would justify God in permitting apparently gratuitous evils. Notice now that Schellenberg's polemical problem of divine hiddenness will have to rest on a principle that is very similar to (GOODS). To see this, return to the direct efforts to resist premise (2) we considered above. Each of these efforts amounted to the suggestion of a reason (rooted either in an evil to be avoided or a good to be secured) that might justify God in permitting reasonable nonbelief. I granted that no single one of these suggested reasons could plausibly be taken by the theist to provide sufficient general grounds for rejecting the conditional premise.[12] Is the failure of each of the efforts to identify a God-justifying reason for the permission of reasonable nonbelief (together with the initial considerations Schellenberg offers in favor of the conditional claim) sufficient to stake the theist to premise (2)? I think not. And this is because it is appropriate for the theist to be skeptical about the principle that would have to be called upon to support the inference to premise (2). In a manner very similar to the evidential argument's dependence on Rowe's inference, the polemical problem of divine hiddenness depends on a noseeum inferential move from

(A) No sufficient reasons we have been able to ascertain can justify a loving God in permitting reasonable nonbelief.

to

(B) There are no sufficient reasons that could justify a loving God in permitting reasonable nonbelief.[13]

I claim that any theist who has already been impressed by the skeptical response to Rowe's argument will be in a strong position to deploy a parallel strategy here.[14]

Let's remind ourselves that a noseeum inference is valid when it is safe to assume that we would see the thing that we do not in fact see *if the thing were there*. So, should the theist accept the noseeum inference of (B) from (A)? Only if it would be reasonable for the theist to think that we would probably be able to recognize God's sufficient reasons for permitting reasonable nonbelief if there were such justifying reasons. That is, the theist should accept the inference only if she first accepts:

(REASONS) If there were reasons sufficient to justify a loving God in permitting reasonable nonbelief, we would probably know about them.

But it seems that we should be as skeptical about (REASONS) as we are about (GOODS). The same intellectual humility with respect to the plans, purposes, and powers of infinite loving wisdom that led us to skepticism about the goods that would justify God in permitting evils like E1 and E2 ought to lead us to be similarly skeptical about the reasons God might have for permitting reasonable nonbelief. I conclude, then, that the skeptical theistic response to the polemical argument from divine hiddenness is just as successful as it is in response to the evidential argument from evil.[15]

4.5　Going Deeper: Relationship and Belief

Consider now a defensive maneuver in response to Schellenberg's argument that the theist might deploy either independently or in concert with the posture of skeptical theism. Specifically, let's return our attention to the conditional premise (2). According to this premise, reasonable nonbelief is incompatible with the existence of a perfectly loving God. The efforts to resist this premise that we canvassed earlier functioned by attempting to demonstrate that the theist has good reasons to conclude that the premise is false. Either in virtue of the plausible existence of goods God could secure only by allowing reasonable nonbelief or in virtue of the plausible existence of evils God could avoid only by allowing reasonable nonbelief, it is rational for the theist to conclude that the forms of unbelief we find in the world are not incompatible with the existence of a loving God. However, we also saw the problems with these brands of defense. Another approach to resisting premise (2) that can avoid these problems will involve challenging the soundness of the sub-argument Schellenberg musters in support of it.

Why, again, does Schellenberg think that his conditional premise is true? His conviction appears to rest on an argument we can express like this:

(1′)　A perfectly loving God will always make it possible for capable human beings to be in intimate reciprocal divine relationship.

(2′)　One can have an intimate reciprocal relationship with another person only if one believes that the other person exists.

(3′)　Therefore, a perfectly loving God will always make it possible for capable human beings to believe that God exists – which is just to say that if a perfectly loving God exists, then reasonable nonbelief does not occur; premise (2) is true.

Now, must the theist accept premises (1′) and (2′) of this sub-argument? I do not think so. In fact, I think there are quite general reasons to reject (2′). Contrary to Schellenberg's crucial assumption, it simply isn't true that the relevant kind of relationship with a person can be enjoyed only by someone who believes that the person exists.

Suppose my wife, Lori, disappears under nefarious circumstances. The evidence I have strongly indicates that she has been kidnapped and murdered (fill in the details for yourself, if you don't mind – I'm not really in the mood to cook up the evidence for the kidnapping and murder of my beloved wife). But now suppose that a month after her disappearance, I get a short email putatively from "her" on a private account. In it, "she" tells me that she is being held (for reasons she can't figure out) but that she has this brief and sneaky access to a computer. She goes on to tell me that she anticipates being able to get brief moments like this one from time to time, during which she will be able to keep up some ongoing correspondence. I realize that this may very well be a hoax, just a way of dragging out my pain or getting further information from me useful to the purposes of the murderers. In fact, let's suppose that my evidence still continues to support the thesis that Lori is dead to such a degree that I am not able to believe she is in fact alive; the new evidence provided by the email correspondence isn't strong enough to support the thesis that she is alive. At best, let's assume, the epistemically rational thing to do, given the total body of my evidence, is withhold judgment about whether Lori is alive.[16] It seems clear to me that, under these conditions, I ought to engage in the email correspondence. At worst, I would not be behaving irrationally in doing so. Now, suppose I do engage in the correspondence and that it goes on for some period of time – say six months. Furthermore, suppose that, in fact, it really *is* Lori on the other end of the correspondence. I am powerfully inclined to conclude that Lori and I will have been in intimate reciprocal relationship for those six months, and this despite the fact that, during this time, I never quite come to believe that Lori is actually alive.[17] I engage in the correspondence, no doubt, in the *hope* that she is alive, but never get evidence sufficient to justify *believing* this. If this scenario is coherent, then premise (2′) is false and the argument for the crucial conditional premise of Schellenberg's main argument is unsupported.

The proponent of the hiddenness argument might reply by attempting to shift the burden back onto the opponent of the argument. She might ask, that is, why God doesn't make straightforward belief possible for everyone, even if a path to reciprocal relationship that does not require belief is also available. There are two things to say in response, and both challenge the idea that the theist must accept this new burden of showing God's reasons for permitting nonbelief even when reciprocal relationship can be had without belief. First, the initially plausible justification for being concerned about unbelief arose from reflection on the value of intimate reciprocal relationship. If it is plausible that such relationship can occur in the absence of belief, then it seems that Schellenbergians will need to reformulate the hiddenness argument around the distinctive value (if there is any) of the kind of relationship (if there is one) that requires belief. Before this reformulation has been offered, it isn't clear that the theist has anything to which to respond. Second, even if we suppose that a reformulation of the proper sort can be achieved, the response of skeptical theism is, once again, going to be quite forceful at this point. Why, you ask, does God permit nonbelief (though reciprocal relationship is nevertheless made possible)? Who knows? And our ignorance about this is precisely what we should have expected. I emphasize once more (and it won't be the last time, I'm afraid) that if the skeptical response has succeeded at the earlier points in this discussion, then it is bound to succeed here as well.

4.6 Going Deeper: Rowe's Complaint about the Parent Analogy

As we saw at the end of chapter 3, though, there may be an especially sharp extension of the hiddenness argument that demands further attention. A crucial animating element of the general strategy of skeptical theism has been the parent analogy. Just as a young cancer-stricken child may be unable to recognize or appreciate the reasons her parent is acting upon in electing to subject her to chemotherapy, so we may be unable to apprehend the reasons God has for permitting the evils we encounter in the world. Recall that in response to this analogy, Rowe has pressed a forceful reply. When a good parent must allow her child to be subjected to suffering that is justified by considerations the child is incapable of understanding, the parent makes a special effort to be close to the child in the midst of the suffering and to communicate comforting messages in a manner the child *can* understand. The suggestion, then, is that at the very least those who suffer for reasons that are beyond their ken should find that God is particularly transparent and close to them. They should experience the divine analogue of the parent's firm embrace and tender words of love and assurance that all will be well. Sadly, it certainly seems like many people endure the gravest hardships without anything like the comforting presence of God. Rowe concludes, therefore, that the parent analogy actually contributes to the case for atheism rather than to the case for theism.

With the polemical problem of hiddenness now before us, we are in position to think of Rowe's response to the parent analogy as a version, or extension, of Schellenberg's argument. Call suffering the justification for which a sufferer is unable to understand "inscrutable" suffering. And call suffering that is endured without the putatively requisite awareness, on the part of the sufferer, of God's presence and love "uncomforted" suffering. This will make it reasonable to think of "uncomforted inscrutable suffering" as a special case of divine hiddenness. Then perhaps Rowe's complaint can be expressed as a version of Schellenberg's argument by replacing premises (2) and (3) with:

(2*) If a perfectly loving God exists, then uncomforted inscrutable suffering does not occur.
(3*) Uncomforted inscrutable suffering occurs.

We end up, obviously, with the same conclusion: that a perfectly loving God does not exist.

But (2*) will have to be supported by a principle parallel to (REASONS) – something like:

(REASONS*) If there were reasons sufficient to justify a loving God in permitting uncomforted inscrutable suffering, we would probably know about them.

And surely by now the skeptical theistic response is getting tiresome even if it is appropriate. Still, it should be clear enough that anyone who has sensible doubts about (GOODS) and (REASONS) will have similarly sensible doubts about (REASONS*). A healthy and rational intellectual humility ought to give us all pause about thinking we have got what it takes to track the mind of God and the nearly infinitely complex interlocking web of values and constraints operative in the divine project of creating a world like our own.

4.7   Conclusion

Here at the conclusion of this chapter and, more generally, at the conclusion of my efforts to offer a set of defenses in response to the problems of evil canvassed in these three chapters, we should remind ourselves about the limits of defense. As a set of *defenses* of the rationality of theistic belief in the light of the full panoply of evils in this world and the hiddenness of God, the responses offered to this point cannot silence the problems we are addressing. At best, they can lower their volume to such a degree that theistic commitment can reasonably be maintained. Perhaps this is the best we can hope for in light of the seriousness of evil and the deep philosophical intractability of the issues it raises (though we will go on in the next chapter at least to explore the possibility of going beyond defense to theodicy).

Furthermore, this is as good a place as any to express what reservations I have about the defensive appeal formalized in the strategy of skeptical theism that has played such a prominent role throughout the past two chapters. As I conceive of these reservations, they do not amount to a reason to reject the strategy, but rather indicate that further work can be done to make the strategy more satisfying. The problem, as I argued in chapter 2, is not that adopting the posture of skeptical theism will force upon us a wider and clearly unacceptable skepticism. Instead, the main issue is that the strategy would seem to force the conclusion that *no* kind, amount, or distribution of evil could *ever* seriously evidentially threaten the theistic belief of the skeptical theist. And this seems like far too strong a conclusion.

What I mean is this. The most thoughtful versions of the challenge for theism from the existence of evil aim to show that evils like E1, E2, and reasonable nonbelief are *some* good evidence that God does not exist. Recall Rowe's emphasis in his characterization of the challenge he takes himself to be making: "Putting aside whatever reasons there may be to think that the theistic God exists, the facts about evil in our world provide good reason to think that God does not exist" (Howard-Snyder et al. 2001, 136). Given this image of the challenge, what the skeptical theist purports to be showing is that we should not – contrary to Rowe, Schellenberg, et al. – take the evils we encounter as good evidence that God does not exist. Now, if you are inclined to think that literally *no* amount of evil or *no* kind of evil or *no* distribution of evil could ever constitute good evidence for the non-existence of God, then you will not be puzzled by the same concern I have. However, I suspect that most will join me in thinking that, even if the evils we actually find in the world presently do not add up to a good reason for atheism, we can at the least imagine circumstances in which they would.

For example, suppose that the world was such that all sentient beings, including intelligent ones like human beings, came into existence only for a very short period of time (say, fifteen minutes), during which they possessed their full mature capacities, throughout which their conscious awareness was totally overwhelmed by excruciating pain on the level of un-anesthetized breach childbirth, and at the end of which the being died and ceased forever to exist. Though the fifteen minutes of tormented life would not likely give the human beings in this world much time or opportunity to reflect on the problem of evil, I think we should conclude that the evil in a world like *that* would indeed be quite good evidence that God did not exist. However, it isn't clear how the proponent of the skeptical theistic response can allow that this is true. That is, even in excruciating world (let's call it), the skeptical theistic defense will seem to work – if it works for a world like ours. After all, just as it would be sensible for us to admit that we are in the dark about what reasons God would have for permitting E1, E2, and reasonable nonbelief in our world, it would seem to be sensible for us to admit that we are in the dark about what reasons God would have for permitting the sufferings of excruciating world. It strikes me as a problem for skeptical theism that this strategy could be successfully deployed even in excruciating world.[18] But perhaps I can say something briefly about why I do not take this problem to constitute a decisive objection to the strategy of skeptical theism.

Two considerations seem to me to count against taking this worry as a general reason to reject the strategy of skeptical theism. First, however antecedently implausible the claim that there might be a morally sufficient justification beyond our ken for God's permission of the suffering of excruciating world (and keep in mind that some theists will simply bite this bullet), the parallel claim that there is a morally sufficient justification beyond our ken for the actual suffering of our world is not nearly as antecedently implausible. This is to say that, independently of the implications of the skeptical response for excruciating world, it continues to appear quite reasonable to remain agnostic on the question of whether God's permission of the evils we actually encounter could be justified by considerations beyond our ken.

Secondly, to press this complaint against the skeptical theist is to open oneself up to a fairly compelling *tu quoque* reply (cf. McBrayer forthcoming). To see this, consider a world much further down the scale of suffering from our own in the opposite direction from excruciating world. Call this world "itch world." In it sentient beings, and intelligent ones like human beings in particular, experience the full scope of pleasures and no pains – other than a few of the human beings who, unfortunately, suffer the itching effects of a minor rash, on the order of what you and I sometimes experi-ence with a mosquito bite. Now, I will grant that there would be some perversity in the skeptical theist pressing her strategy in the face of the evils of excruciating world. "Surely," we are tempted to say, "*that* amount and kind of suffering is strong evidence for the non-existence of God." The critic of the skeptical approach may find herself leaping to the reply that skeptical theism, therefore, fails *simpliciter* since it fails for excruciating world. But notice a parallel perversity that would seem to supervene on the same thought: namely, the perversity of pressing the problem of evil in itch world. "Surely," we are tempted to say, "*that* amount and kind of suffering is *not* strong evidence for the non-existence of God." And if the critic of skeptical theism is justified in concluding that the skeptical response fails generally by virtue of failing at excruciating world, then it seems that the argument from evil for atheism also fails generally by virtue of failing at itch world. Of course, this doesn't show precisely how the skeptical theist can make the skeptical appeal with respect to the evils of the actual world and still think that the evils of excruciating world would provide good grounds for rejecting theism. Some philosophical work remains to be done. So be it.[19]

Furthermore and finally, even if the general defensive efforts I have made over the past three chapters are successful and demonstrate that the thoughtful theist is within her rights in maintaining her belief despite the kinds, amounts, and distribution of evil (including reasonable nonbelief) we actually face, it would not be unreasonable for the theist to long for something more than the piecemeal parrying of atheistic attacks that have occupied us thus far. The theist may want not merely to avoid the blows but to decisively end the fight. She may want, that is, to produce a positive theodicy.

5
The Project of Theodicy

When Gottfried Wilhelm Leibniz coined the term "Theodicy" for the title of his book (the subtitle of which is *On the Goodness of God, the Freedom of Man, and the Origin of Evil*), he seems to have had in mind the very general project of demonstrating that God (*theos*) is just (*dike*) in allowing the evil we find in the world. Less than fifty years after the publication of this book, the Lisbon earthquake of 1755 gave Voltaire a profound hammer with which to brutalize the project. Both in his satirical novel *Candide* and in his "Poem on the Lisbon Disaster," Voltaire used the earthquake as the cornerstone of his attack on the idea, central to Leibniz's argument in *Theodicy*, that this is the best of all possible worlds. Without question, the Lisbon earthquake did seem to come ready-made for Voltaire's use. The earthquake was remarkably violent – we suppose it would have registered 8.5 or more on the Richter scale – and its consequences were almost equal parts disastrous and ironic. The ironies: it struck a deeply Catholic city, on All Saints Day, and failed to do much damage to the city's red-light district while destroying most of its churches (robbing apologists of any real force for the argument that it was the result of God's judgment for the city's sinfulness). The disasters: tens of thousands were killed by the earthquake itself and by the tsunami and fires that followed, and eighty-five percent of the buildings in Lisbon were destroyed (including, for further irony, the recently completed Phoenix Opera House, which – wait for it – burned to the ground). It would have been interesting to see how Leibniz would have framed a second edition of his *Theodicy* if he had lived to see the Lisbon earthquake and its aftermath, both philosophical and otherwise.

I will remind you, however, that our goal is not to survey the history of various treatments of the problem of evil. Our target is the current debate. So, although we owe the terminology of "theodicy" to Leibniz, we will now put him and his enlightenment critics aside to turn our attention to the contemporary discussion. And to do this well we will need to remind ourselves of the more precise account of theodicy we introduced in the first chapter. A theodicy, on this more careful rendering of the project, goes beyond a defense, which has the limited goal of showing only that a particular argument from evil for atheism has not been demonstrably successful. It goes beyond a defense, as we said before, by seeking to show what God's morally sufficient reasons for permitting evil might very well be – that is, what they can reasonably be thought to be. The reason that this precision is necessary is because there are two popular ways of understanding theodicy, both of which we will be denying ourselves here. On the one hand, theodicy is sometimes thought of as *any* effort to address one or another of the problems of evil. The contemporary philosophical debate has generally rejected this use of the terminology, however, because it is too general. In particular, it can make it difficult for us to mark off the project of defense as importantly different from the project we will take up in this chapter.[1] On the other hand, theodicy is sometimes characterized as the human effort to provide God's *actual* reasons for permitting the evils in the world. This way of thinking of theodicy, however, makes it a project that no one ought to be much tempted to take up. Who has the hubris to insist that he is in a position to ascertain God's actual reasons? Instead, then, our use of the terminology of theodicy will characterize a project that is specific enough to distinguish it from defense and humble enough to be satisfied with providing reasons that *would* justify God in permitting evil – even though it stops short of insisting that these are God's actual reasons for doing so.

Still, the project of theodicy understood in this way (which is more or less the canonical way of understanding it in contemporary philosophy of religion) remains quite a bold undertaking even if – and this is still contentious – it stops short of outright hubris. This is because, unlike defenses, the central commitments of a successful theodicy cannot merely be possibly true or even true for all we know. Rather, the central commitments will have to be *plausibly* true – reasonably likely to be true.

To be somewhat more specific, at the heart of any theodicy is the judgment that there are goods so valuable that they can *plausibly* be thought to justify God in seeking to secure them – even at the cost of the world's horrors. A successful theodicy will, then, have to make it reasonable to believe *both* that the target goods really are so valuable as to justify the existence of horrible evils *and* that there was no way for God to secure these goods without causing or permitting the evils. That is, a theodicy must offer plausible support for two claims:

- *The Value Claim*: A world containing these (or comparable) goods and these (or comparable) evils is better than any world containing neither.
- *The Impossibility Claim*: It was impossible for God to secure a world containing these (or comparable) goods without it also containing these (or comparable) evils.

Now, the fact of the matter is that there are countless theodicies. We don't have the space to do anything close to surveying them all. Instead, what we can do is look briefly at a set of the most prominent and plausible goods that contemporary philosophers of religion have offered to fill in the value and impossibility claims above. In no case can any one of these supposed goods plausibly function alone as an explanation for God's permission of all the evils we encounter. Instead, different theodicies have emphasized different sets of these goods (and others that we will simply have to ignore) in unique proportions and interrelations. What we have the space to consider are only the principle *ingredients* in influential contemporary theodicies. You will have to explore the more specific recipes on your own.[2]

5.1   The Value of Free Will

Nearly every contemporary attempt at theodicy appeals to the unique value of robust human free will. As we saw with Plantinga's Free Will Defense, it is initially quite plausible to suppose that beings lacking free will would be neither intrinsically nor extrinsically as valuable as beings possessing it. It does indeed seem intrinsically good for creatures to be able to deliberate about courses of action and to be able to direct their own wills on the basis of this deliberation without being compelled to make a particular decision by external forces – whether of nature or nurture. Furthermore, there are important arguments linking our capacities as free beings with our status as distinctively *moral* beings. So it is reasonable to suppose that free will is required for any being to be properly regarded as morally responsible for how it behaves. It wouldn't be unreasonable to worry, then, that without free will either there would be no morality or the deepest strains of morality would be lost. In addition, many proponents of theodicy have drawn attention to the supposedly special kind of relationship that could occur between God and creatures only if the creatures enter into the relationship of their own free will and not as a result of divine coercion or manipulation.

All of this is to say that free will can at least initially be thought to function as one of (or as a necessary condition for some of) the goods figuring in a theodicist's defense of the plausibility of the *value claim*. What, however, about the *impossibility claim*? How plausible is the suggestion that not even an omnipotent being could bring about a world containing the good of human freedom without also bringing about a world containing evils of the kinds and in the amounts we find? For this suggestion to have even the smell of plausibility, it seems that the kind of freedom in question will have to be of the incompatibilist variety also emphasized by Plantinga in his defense. This is because it is very difficult to see why an omnipotent being should face an insurmountable challenge when tasked with making a world in which creatures were free in the compatibilist sense and who also never engaged in the gruesome forms of wrongdoing that bring about the lion's share of human suffering. Recall that, according to compatibilism, a person can be free even if she is causally determined, even if everything she does happens necessarily as the result of antecedent circumstances and the laws of nature. This means that if compatibilism is true, then God could have made beings who were free but who were nevertheless guaranteed always to act according to the divine will. God could have causally determined them to act well without having any negative impact on their freedom. There is no conceptual or logical problem here and, therefore, no impossibility for omnipotence. So even if we grant that free will is distinctively valuable in all the ways considered above, the relevant form of freedom must be of the incompatibilist sort in order for the impossibility claim to be even initially plausible.

In the case of the free will defense, it was enough for Plantinga that incompatibilism about free will is *possibly* true. But the proponent of theodicy, as we have been emphasizing, must go further to show that her premises are *likely* to be true. With respect to theodicies that depend on the value of incompatibilist free will (which is, again, almost all of them), then, it is incumbent upon their proponents to make a forceful case for the plausibility of our possessing this form of freedom. That is, the theodicist must make a compelling argument for the truth of libertarianism. This is no small task. The majority of contemporary philosophers, as we had occasion to mention in chapter 2, favor either compatibilism or skepticism about free will, the acceptance of either of which will undermine a free will theodicy. And there are a number of important arguments intended to show that the brand of free will associated with libertarianism is either incoherent or wildly unsupported by our evidence.[3] In short, then, the free will theodicist must not duck the task of defending the appeal to incompatibilism – as, I think, some have.[4]

Return now to the value claim. Though I allowed that free will has some initial claim to a kind of importance that would justify God in seeking to preserve it at the cost of the world's evils, a satisfying theodicy will have to make the case on this point with considerable force. To see the challenge, note that a recurring complaint made against libertarianism by compatibilists is that the view is simply unmotivated. That is, these critics regularly insist that nothing of real value turns on whether the kind of freedom we possess is (or is not) compatible with thoroughgoing determinism. This is at least part of the point of the subtitle of Daniel Dennett's influential book *Elbow Room: The Varieties of Free Will Worth Wanting* (1984). But it isn't only compatibilists who have raised questions about just how valuable libertarian freedom really is. Derk Pereboom, a self-described "hard-incompatibilist," has developed an extended defense of the thesis that human beings do not possess free will (of either the compatibilist or libertarian sort) but that this is not so bad – because nothing much is lost in our giving up on free will. In particular, he argues that we can keep much of morality, of law and punishment, of interpersonal relationships, and of the meaning of our lives (2001). Pereboom does admit that we will not be able to keep *everything* we may want if we give up on free will; and, therefore, there is space for the proponent of a free will theodicy to make the case for distinctive value. But the case needs to be made, and it needs to be made in such a way that the value of libertarian free will can be seen to outstretch the value of its denial *significantly*, since it is in part this additional value that is supposed to be justifying God in permitting much of the evil parasitic upon this freedom.

Finally, we shouldn't ignore just how limited the appeal to free will is likely to be in a full accounting for the world's evils. A great many of the evils we face seem to have nothing whatsoever to do with the choices of free creatures, falling as many of them do in the category of natural evils.

5.2 The Value of Soul-Making

Another important ingredient in nearly every contemporary theodicy is an appeal to the concept of "soul-making." The prominence of this theme in the current debate is due largely to John Hick's extensive development of the concept in his influential book *Evil and the God of Love* (1978). The core thought is deeply teleological; that is, it turns crucially on the divine purposes for human beings. God is aiming to bring into existence that immeasurably good state in which free and rational creatures are in the richest possible intimacy with their Creator. According to Hick, this is a state that we can only enter into *freely*; thus the importance of libertarian freedom, as we have already emphasized. But, in addition, Hick claims that this is a state that we can only enter into if we are deeply good – only if our souls have undergone the proper transformation.[5] Now, this deep goodness is, according to Hick, *essentially* developmental. It is not the sort of goodness that one could have simply implanted in one or in the possession of which one could arise out of the swamp. This means that, insofar as God's worthy goal is to give creatures the opportunity to cooperate with divinity in achieving this highly prized goodness, God will have to place them in an environment that includes genuine moral obstacles and risk. On the assumption, then, that God is seeking to develop moral saints rather than to guarantee a certain amount of pleasure, the question for theodicy shifts. Initially, it may have seemed that our question was, "Does human existence have enough pleasure to be permitted by a maximally loving being?" Now we can see, however, that the question must be something more like, "Is the world as we find it a reasonable moral training ground?" Hick attempts to provide a plausible positive answer to this question.

As he emphasizes, both pain and suffering will have to be live possibilities in this training ground. Pain appears to be necessary as the principal biological mechanism for getting creatures like us to care about the exercise of our own capacities and the development of our skills. Without pain (think of hunger pangs or the pains of disease and aging), we would have no reason to seek food, cultivate the land, invent medications, or take on temporally extended projects requiring planning, willpower, and teamwork. Without pain, "[t]here would be," Hick claims, "nothing to avoid and nothing to seek; no occasion for cooperation or mutual help; no stimulus to the development of culture or the creation of civilization" (1978, 343). Suffering more generally appears to be required for the instantiation of the most robust moral concepts like cruelty, injustice, and unfaithfulness (on the negative side) and courage, compassion, and perseverance (on the positive side). Our free decisions between such serious options make our deep moral character, for good or ill: the possibility of the ill being a necessary consequence of the possibility of the good.

If something like this is right, then the proponent of a soul-making theodicy will have some sensible things to say in support of the value and impossibility claims. Surely our entering into the deepest kind of relationship with God is an immensely valuable state of affairs. Intuitively, a world with the possibility of this kind of human/divine intimacy is better than worlds without it (though maybe it matters just how likely it is that the possibility will be realized). And if Hick is right about the essentially developmental nature of the deep goodness necessary for this intimacy, then it would be reasonable to conclude that there is a logical obstacle to the creation of a world with the intimacy but without the evils necessary for the development. We should add that, unlike the appeal to free will, the appeal to soul-making can go at least some distance toward a plausible justification for the existence of distinctively natural evils. Without some of them, it would seem, we would not be able to develop the forms of moral character that God aims to cultivate in us.

Once again, the value of soul-making cannot by itself ground a satisfying theodicy. Hick grants that we also need incompatibilist free will. But even the values of free will and soul-making taken together won't close the explanatory gap between divine goodness and actual evil. This is because there appear to be instances of suffering in our world that bear no relationship to the building of souls. Rowe's suffering fawn was designed precisely to be a prototypical case in point, and the vast array of animal suffering in general puts considerable pressure on the plausibility of the soul-making account. In addition, there appear to be instances of suffering that are so powerful or so pointed as to *destroy* souls rather than give them a context for development. In addition to the cases of senseless and unredeemed torture (of children, for example – and, again, Rowe's choice of cases is no accident), we should think deeply, if painfully, about the effects of profound mental illness in this regard. Part of the horror of profound mental illness is that it twists the human psyche in such a way that it seems no moral growth can be taken from it by the one who suffers under it.

The continuing challenge for the proponent of a soul-making theodicy is, then, at least two-fold. First, she must accommodate the apparent existence of forms of suffering that transcend any plausible purposes of moral or spiritual growth.[6] Second, she must defend the claim that a world with the horrendous evils we actually encounter and, therefore, with the robust possibility of deep moral goodness really is better than a world without the possibility of such goodness but also without the horrors.

5.3   The Value of Stable Natural Laws

The final standard ingredient in contemporary theodicies that we will consider is an appeal to the value of fixed and elegant laws of nature. In some philosophical moods, probably a great many of us can be talked into the idea that there is an intrinsic metaphysical excellence to a world governed by laws that strike a sexy balance between simplicity and extension. A broad and coherent swathe of natural phenomena unified by a small set of simple rules is, arguably, a beautiful thing. A number of philosophers have also pointed out the instrumental value of a world governed in this way (cf. Swinburne 1998; van Inwagen 2006). Without fixed and coherent laws of nature, the kinds of moral action that soul-making requires would be impossible. If you are going to save someone from drowning, for example, the laws of nature will have to be regular and predictable – in order for there to *be* danger, in order for you to *recognize* the danger, and in order for you to *execute* your rescue plan. In addition, as Richard Swinburne has emphasized, it looks as if uniform laws are necessary for our robust epistemic access to the world. To the degree that inquiry and knowledge are good, a world conducive to them is as well. And a conducive world will have to be one unified by coherent laws. Unfortunately, it looks as if a world governed by laws of this sort will almost inevitably also contain the suffering of creatures that are subject to them. Fixed laws make responsible action and valuable knowledge possible, but they also necessarily make real danger possible. So, once again, the appeal to stable laws has a chance of supporting both the value claim and the impossibility claim. With respect to the impossibility claim in particular, we should note that the appeal to the value of stable natural laws provides for at least an initially plausible response to the question of why God doesn't alleviate a great deal more suffering in the world by way of saving miracles. The answer is that a world with miracles occurring too frequently and transparently would be one in which we could not come to learn about or depend on the laws of nature in the ways required for our moral and spiritual development. We would not recognize the dangers – say, of smoking, of letting our children cross freeways, or of climbing mountains without proper equipment – if divine miracles regularly saved us from the consequences of these activities. Similarly, we could not leverage our decisions into compassionate and courageous help if regular divine interventions veiled not just the dangers but also the efficacy of our wills.

Again, and obviously enough, the value of stable laws alone will not provide an especially firm foundation for theodicy. Appeal to it cannot give us much of an account of the existence of moral evil generally, for example. But taken in concert with the values of free will and soul-making, the value of stable laws does appear to make some contribution. In fact, Peter van Inwagen has argued that appeal to the value of stable laws can help to account for the suffering of non-human animals that, as we have already had occasion to note, goes largely ignored by free will and soul-making theodicists (2006). According to van Inwagen, it may very well be that any world containing high-level sentient creatures like us would either have to be subject to the kinds of suffering we find (particularly among animals) or be "massively irregular." A massively irregular world is one in which the laws of nature are a long way from the kind of elegant simplicity we seem to find them possessing in our world – and against the background of which, as we've just been saying, various moral and spiritual goods could emerge. Massive irregularity, van Inwagen goes on to suggest, would make a world at least as bad as any world containing the kind of suffering we find in ours. The key thought, then, is that any world with stable laws and the emergence of high-level sentient creatures would probably have something like the patterns of animal suffering with which we are sadly familiar.

The problem, however, is that van Inwagen offers his appeal to the disvalue of massively irregular worlds only as a *defense* in the face of arguments from animal suffering. What this means is that van Inwagen defends his central commitments only as *true for all we know*. Nothing we know, he thinks, renders his claims implausible; this would, you will recall, be sufficient for a satisfying defense. However, using his appeal as a feature of a theodicy would require us to show not just that his claims cannot be shown to be *im*plausible but that they are in fact plausible. Can it be shown to be reasonable to believe that (1) no massively irregular world could have contained high-level sentient creatures like human beings, (2) it is very important for the world to contain high-level sentient creatures like human beings, and (3) massive irregularity makes a world worse than does the suffering (including all the animal suffering) we find in ours? Maybe. But also maybe not. It strikes me, at least, as *prima facie* tricky to render (1) and (3) straightforwardly plausible, as a theodicy deploying the value of stable laws to account for animal suffering would have to do.

The values of free will, soul-making, and stable laws of nature are, as I have emphasized already, only a subset of those that could be called upon to support a theodicy. Perhaps there are additional goods (for example, of creatures being of use, of humans being able to do both great harm and great good, of morally guilty creatures being properly punished for their wrongdoing, to name just a few) that would also contribute to a case for the plausibility of the value and impossibility claims.[7] I hope that our brief reflection on the three principal and popular values can give you some initial sense of the structure and viability of the contemporary project of theodicy.

5.4 Eschatological Optimism?

Beyond the principal values on which a theodicy will have to be built, it is also nearly inevitable that the proponent of theodicy will be forced to take a stand on eschatological questions about how things will ultimately turn out for God's creatures. The theodicist, that is, will not be able to ignore the nature of the afterlife and matters of heaven and hell. The reason should be clear enough. Natural human lives and, in fact, the cosmos itself appear to be finite in temporal extension. If neither we nor the world are going to last forever, then it seems that whatever values are going to be called upon to justify God in permitting evil will have to do their justificatory work within the limited time frame of finitude. It would seem to help the project of theodicy, however, if we could count on an afterlife characterized by new kinds, amounts, and distributions of goods – goods that might very well render the sufferings of the present world essentially insignificant by comparison. Theodicy would surely be easier to do from the point of view of heaven. Unfortunately, the converse also appears to be true regarding hell. If some really are damned to an eternal state of unmitigated suffering, then it will be particularly difficult to render the value and impossibility claims plausible.

So just how optimistic about the eschatological future for human beings must a promising theodicy be? This is a matter of considerable (and vibrant) contemporary discussion. On the most optimistic end of the spectrum are those who insist that a plausible story of God's permission of all the evils in the world will have to include universalism – which is the view that every human being will eventually join the redeemed in heaven in the beatific vision of God. No one is ultimately hell-bound. Hick reached this conclusion with regard to his theodicy. Given that the central value justifying God's permission of the world's evils is the good of each free creature developing into the kind of person capable of cooperative divine intimacy, and given that very few people (if any) appear to reach this level of development in the course of their natural lives, God must provide life beyond life in order to finish this work. Furthermore, Hick argues that God's permission of the profound evils of our world could only be justified by the concrete realization of the end of the teleological process: namely, the maximal good of *every* free creature ultimately reaching the end-state of unbridled intimacy with God. Anything less, he thinks, would leave some of the suffering of our world unjustified. Marilyn Adams reaches the same eschatologically optimistic conclusion for related reasons (1993, 1999).

Richard Swinburne defends his theodicy in less eschatologically optimistic terms. He claims that if people have formed their character well, then "they will have a natural propensity to show gratitude and respect when it is due, and so be ready to worship their creator, if they learn of his existence." And he grants that "[t]hey may not have that opportunity until after death" (1998, 257–8). Thus, Swinburne appears to be joining Hick in granting if not the need for, then at least, again, the *possibility* of an eschatological, post-mortem component in his theodicy. The less optimistic feature of Swinburne's theodicy is this: he appears to accept that God could remain perfectly good even while granting to a human being only a limited temporal opportunity to make a decision about her eternal destiny. In fact, God's goodness may require this, because anything less would amount to a failure to give our wills their proper respect.

> For if God refused to allow someone to develop an irreformably bad character, that would be depriving her of an ultimate choice of the sort of person she is to be. If God always left the bad open to good influences, that would be refusing to recognize an ultimate choice by an independent moral agent. (1998, 121)

This does not entail, for Swinburne, a traditional doctrine of hell, however, since it is compatible with God's causing some people to pass out of existence altogether. Given many of the things he says about this, it would not be terribly uncharitable to describe his preferred view as something like annihilationism. Thus, while Swinburne allows for extended post-mortem soul-building – especially for compensation when a particular human being has not received a fair share of goodness in earthly life – there is an ultimate limit on it.

Eleonore Stump has made the most forceful effort to defend the compatibility of divine goodness with a more or less traditional doctrine of hell as a place of eternal suffering for its denizens. The challenge she takes up is to show how even hell could be an expression of divine love. Leaning on insights she gleans from both Thomas Aquinas and Dante, she argues that hell may be the only loving way for God to respect the two fundamental values that are in tension here. On the one hand, God must honor the free will of creatures who choose not to enter into the beatific vision. On the other hand, God (as perfectly good) cannot destroy that which is intrinsically valuable: namely, the souls of the rebellious. This second point entails that annihilation of the damned would be inconsistent with omnibenevolence. The upshot is that those who freely reject entrance into heaven will still have to be maintained in existence. Must they be tortured by God (or Satan), however? No. On Stump's view, the damned are not so much tortured by external powers as allowed to act in accordance with the characters they have formed by their own free wills. The damned do indeed suffer, then, and eternally. However, their suffering is essentially self-inflicted (cf. Stump 1985, 1986).

I leave it, once again, to you to assess these alternative positions regarding the integration of the afterlife into a successful theodicy.

5.5 Going Deeper: The Evil of Theodicy

We should not ignore a deep thread of complaint about the project of theodicy. There might, after all, be something wrong not merely with particular efforts to produce a theodicy or with specific premises in theodic arguments, but more generally with the *aim* of theodicy itself. What some opponents of theodicy have argued is that we make a grave mistake simply in trying to offer reasons that may justify God in permitting the world's evils. Theodicy, according to the strongest versions of this kind of complaint, is just one more of the world's evils. Why think anything as strong as this? Two broad kinds of considerations have been offered, one moral and the other theological (cf. Trakakis forthcoming).

From the moral point of view, it isn't hard to see the danger of proposing a theodicy. As we have conceived of the project, a theodicy attempts to identify some plausible reasons God may have for allowing the instances of even the most horrible evils our world sadly contains. However, if a theodicy justifies God in allowing these evils, then it seems that these evils (appearances notwithstanding) must not really be as horrible as we thought. Some evils strike us as truly gratuitous – as truly such that there could be no justification for their occurrence. In offering a theodicy for all evil we, in essence, deny that any evils really are gratuitous; we deny that any evils really are quite as bad as we originally perceived them to be. After all, how bad can they really be if God has a good reason for permitting them? The result is that theodicy minimizes evil and blocks us from recognizing the class of suffering that is most disturbing: namely, gratuitous suffering.

Another form of moral complaint about theodicy takes note of the particular way that influential strands of theodicy have appealed to a kind of consequentialist moral reasoning. It has not been uncommon for theodicies to be formulated in terms of the greater goods God preserves or establishes by allowing some to suffer. However, one need not be a full-blown Kantian to object to the treatment of some people as mere means to ends, even divinely ordered ends. This moral complaint about theodicy is, then, that it inevitably involves a picture of God using people in transparently immoral ways, as mere means to the teleological ends of the specific greater goods, whether these ends are the possibility of free choice, the good of soul-making, or what have you.

Theological objections to theodicy often take the form of complaints about the hyper-anthropomorphic conceptions of God that proponents of theodicy take for granted. The point here is not that any anthropomorphism is unacceptable. Almost everyone grants that theism will need to draw various parallels between divine and human agency. Rather, the opponents of theodicy claim to detect ungrounded or naïve anthropomorphic commitments in the efforts to offer justifications for God's permission of evil. As a case in point, some anti-theodicists argue that God is not, contrary to the assumptions of theodicy, one member among others in our moral community. God is not, that is, the kind of being who is subject to morality with its demands and criticisms. Rather, God is, in some sense, beyond these demands and criticisms. But without the assumption that God is a participant in our moral order, theodicy has no point. In fact, engaging in theodicy only serves to ingrain a shallow anthropocentrism into the philosophical debate.

My own view is that there is much to learn from the complaints of the most reasonable opponents of theodicy. In fact, I am convinced that the contemporary debate over the problem of evil is markedly more humane than it would have been without the contributions of those who have worried about the moral and theological implications of theodicy. Nevertheless, the conclusion that seems to me to be justified is not that theodicy *per se* is either morally or theologically unacceptable. Instead, what the complaints provide (again, when they are reasonable) is a set of conditions that an acceptable theodicy must meet. For example, a successful theodicy must not minimize the seriousness of evil or have as a consequence of its commitments that the world's horrors are really not so bad. Furthermore, proponents of theodicy should either vigorously defend a consequentialist meta-ethic or be sure that God is not placed in the role of using human beings as means to divine ends. Finally, theodicists ought to consider the degree to which their arguments presuppose anthropocentric conceptions of God and the divine relationship to morality. However, as I have said, the challenges arising from the anti-theodicy movement can be incorporated into the project of theodicy as reasonable constraints, and need not be taken as knock-down objections to the project itself. Now, some particular efforts at theodicy may indeed be properly criticized as contributing to the world's evils, and precisely for reasons of the kind we have just considered. To conclude on the basis of these cases that any such effort will similarly contribute to the world's evils strikes me, however, as considerably too hasty.

5.6   Going Deeper: The Need for Theodicy

The final substantive issue we will take up in this context has to do with the supposed necessity of theodicy. Must the theist, in order to be epistemically rational, be able to point to something like a successful theodicy? Somewhat famously, when Plantinga first introduced the concept of defense into the contemporary discussion of the problem of evil, he claimed that the theodicies on the table at that time were unacceptable. In fact, he suggested that the project of theodicy should simply be replaced by the project of defense (Tomberlin and van Inwagen 1985, 35). This appeared to be the philosophical sentiment that carried the day for a few decades. It came as some surprise, then, when Richard Swinburne began to argue that for most theists in the modern world, a theodicy (or something near enough) is probably required; without one, he has argued, the rationality of their continued belief is probably undermined.[8] Swinburne's argument for this set of claims turns on both his account of the goals of theodicy and his commitment to a central epistemic principle he refers to as the Principle of Credulity.

As Swinburne sees it, the atheist who presses the problem of evil purports to find in the world cases of badness that either God has no right to allow or are such that God would have done better by not allowing it. In either case, then, these are instances of evil that a maximally good being would not permit. And, therefore, the existence of these evils entails that God does not exist. A Swinburnean theodicy is an effort, on the part of the theist, to demonstrate (to himself) how all the evils we encounter are probably of the sort that could be permitted by a perfectly good being.

But why think that most contemporary theists need such a theodicy in order for their continuing belief in God to be rational? Here is where the Principle of Credulity comes in. According to the Principle of Credulity, if something seems to be the case for us (if we naturally find ourselves with a strong pull to believe it), then barring additional evidence to the contrary, it is probably true. That is, if you feel the strong pull to believe it and you have no defeaters for your belief, then you *should* believe it. Swinburne claims that without accepting something like the Principle of Credulity as the underlying support for our properly basic beliefs, we wouldn't be able to believe anything at all. He goes on to claim, however, with a great deal of sensitivity to our experience with evil in the world, that most of us will have encountered intrinsically bad things that appear to us to be such that either God has no right to allow them to occur or God could have done better by not allowing them. In fact, Swinburne goes even further. Not only does he claim that many of us will face evils for which there appear to us to be no God-justifying reasons; he argues that most of us would exhibit a moral failing in seeing things differently! So it is not just that a great many theists will be struck by evil's apparent unjustifiability in many cases; in addition, most theists who do not have this experience of being so struck are probably morally defective in some way. All of this is to say that Swinburne is deeply committed to the idea that some intrinsically bad events are going to look to us as if there could be no good reason for God to allow them. Given the Principle of Credulity, then, we should believe that there could be no good reason for God to allow them – unless we are presented with counterevidence. Swinburne's theodicy is intended to be this counterevidence. And without it, he believes, the rational thing to conclude would be that there is no God-justifying reason for the evil and, therefore, that God does not exist.

On Swinburne's account, then, the stakes are quite high for theodicy. Should we accept that the stakes really are this high? Should we accept, that is, that the rationality of belief in God for most contemporary theists requires a Swinburnean theodicy? This is an open question worth further exploration. I have my doubts, however, and for two reasons. First, Swinburne himself grants that, in addition to a theodicy of the kind he musters, the rationality of theistic belief could also be insulated from his worry about the appearance of unjustifiable evil by strong independent grounds for believing in the existence of God (1998, 23 and 29). This means the door remains open for something like the Moorean Shift we saw in the context of Rowe's evidential argument. And, pursuing an argument similar to one I offered in that context, if it is true that belief in God can be properly basic, then it may be that the basicality of belief in God could trump the basicality of belief that a particular evil could not be permitted by God. Swinburne grants, as he should, that a corollary of the Principle of Credulity is that the stronger our natural inclination to believe a proposition, the more rational it is for us to do so. Thus, a strong enough inclination to believe that God exists might swamp (and justifiably so) the belief provoked by the encounter with apparently gratuitous evil.

Second, it is not clear to me that very many people either will or should have the "seemings" that Swinburne insists upon. It is no doubt true that many will be horrified by the evils they encounter or hear about, and many will also be struck by the *prima facie* gratuitousness of them. I will even grant that we *should* be so struck. But this is still some inferential distance from the thought that God either has no right to allow these evils or should have eliminated them. What I mean is that it is difficult for me to attribute to a particular horrible event the property of its seeming to me that God could have no good reason to allow it. Certainly I can appreciate there being an argument based on some features of the horrible event to the conclusion that there could be no God-justifying reason for permitting it. But what Swinburne insists upon is the quite natural and common experience of our *seeing* that this is so, rather than our *concluding* that this is so on the basis of other reasons or arguments. By way of analogy, I grant that its seeming to me that there is a book on the table properly grounds my belief that there is a book on the table, in the absence of defeaters. But what should we say about someone to whom it seems that the book on the table could not have been placed there by space aliens with technology wholly unknown to us? Should this person, on the basis of this quite complex supposed seeming, believe according to it in the absence of defeaters? It isn't obvious to me that the answer is yes. The complex seeming to which Swinburne appeals strikes me as more like the second controversial seeming than the first quite ordinary one.

In any case, I think we should conclude that the requirement of a successful theodicy for the rationality of theistic belief has not yet been demonstrated.

5.7 Conclusion

It goes without saying, I trust, that nothing like a comprehensive assessment of theodicy has (or could have) been undertaken here. Still, we have been able to sketch the main contours of important contemporary efforts at systematic theodicy. As you should have expected, I have left out a great deal of detail; in fact, I have simply ignored many substantive issues that deserve attention. There is, of course, much more to be said both for and against contemporary strategies of theodicy.

I will conclude very briefly by parrying, rather than directly answering, what might be thought to be the central question raised by this chapter: namely, can a theodicy succeed? The fact is that I think there can be no simple answer to this question – in large part because the general conditions of success for a theodicy are either unstable or opaque.

Whether a particular deployment of theodicy succeeds depends crucially on what it is supposed to do and by whom it is to be evaluated. Swinburne, for example, is admirably clear about these features of his own project. In defending the need for theodicy, he argues, as we have seen, that it is incumbent upon most theists to offer one in order to be justified in their respective theistic beliefs. What his theodicy must show, he claims, is how (and not merely *that*) it is probably the case that God is morally justified in permitting all the world's evils. Swinburne is explicit that this demonstration must be made only to the subject's own satisfaction, by reference to her own standards of probability, and against the background of justified beliefs she already has.[9] This means that a particular theodicy may succeed for some and not for others. In light of the fairly low and subjective bar Swinburne sets for justification, we should surely conclude that some theodicies will, in fact, succeed for many theists.

But the aims and measures of theodicy proposed by Swinburne are not the only ones there are. Peter van Inwagen, for example, has insisted that a successful philosophical argument, in any domain, would have to convert a court of idealized neutral inquirers under appropriate dialectical circumstances to its conclusion (2006, 47). Applied to theodicy, this would mean that a court of such neutral inquirers would have to be persuaded by it that the considerations adduced are probably sufficient to justify God in permitting the world's evils. This is a much higher bar of success than the one Swinburne sets for himself. It would be hard to be especially optimistic about the prospects of success for any theodicy that accepts the van Inwagen conditions.[10]

Where does this leave us? Not, I hope, with simple cynicism about the project of theodicy or about the prospects for its future development. In addition to being in a better position to understand the structure and liabilities of contemporary theodicies, perhaps we are also now in a better position to evaluate future theodicies in the light of their respective and particular aims.[11]

6
Tentative Conclusions and Beyond

In the opening chapter of this book, I suggested that the human encounter with evil in its various forms has the power to draw us in two opposing directions. Some, following Ivan Karamazov, are drawn by it toward skepticism and unbelief. Others – like the ridiculous man of Dostoevsky's short story – are drawn by it into faith and commitment. We shouldn't pretend that either of these characteristically human responses enjoys the undiluted support of pure rationality. In whichever direction we feel pulled by our own experiences with the world's horrors, the particular gravitational field in which we find ourselves is bound to be at least partly a function of psychological and sociological influences that have little to do with the (so-called) force of the better argument. As I hope has been clear, my primary goal throughout this book has been to animate and explain the central arguments offered in the contemporary debate among analytic philosophers of religion regarding the problem of evil. If I have succeeded on this score, then you will now be in position to appreciate these arguments, weigh them intelligently, and enter into this important and subtle debate yourself.

However, I have also pursued a secondary goal in a way, I hope, that has been in the service of the primary one. This secondary goal has been to argue for the basic rationality of theistic belief despite the challenges presented by the various problems of evil. In essence, then, I have been attempting to show that the response of Dostoevsky's ridiculous man is not inherently ridiculous and that reason does not necessarily oppose the pull toward belief that some of us sometimes feel in the face of suffering and tragedy. With respect to this secondary goal, I will make one last argument in this concluding chapter. With respect to the primary goal, it will be valuable for us to take final note of some elements of the problems of evil we have left essentially unexplored and to reconsider the limitation we have placed on ourselves to respond to the problems of evil from the standpoint of common theism.

6.1   A Problem of Evil for Atheism

However you are inclined to assess the replies to the problems of evil available to the theist, there is no question that evil *is* a problem for theism. That is, evil raises a real worry about the intellectual viability of theism. It might be tempting to think that the atheist faces a parallel problem – a problem of good. How might this parallel problem be framed? Well, perhaps there is an inconsistency, either logical or evidential, between the claim that God does not exist and the obvious truth that our world is marked by instances of goodness. The only way I can see to make this temptation into anything more substantial would be by showing that the very concept of goodness cannot be reasonably supported by atheism. If, for example, there were powerful reasons to accept a meta-ethical view according to which there could be (or would very likely be) no goodness without God, then this kind of parallel argument might have some teeth. By my lights, however, this is not a very promising line of argument. As a theist myself, I am naturally inclined to think that God will have something to do with the foundations of morality and the fundamental nature of goodness. Indeed, I generally find that the extant accounts of morality without God leave out important elements of our common ethical experience and cast it in an unattractive light (a point I will try to take advantage of shortly). But I am sufficiently impressed with the coherence and plausibility of naturalistic theories of morality and value not to be very confident that a compelling inconsistency or implausibility can be turned upon atheism from this perspective. So it isn't clear to me that atheism has some parallel problem of good – at least not one that could be made precise without a lifetime of philosophical work on the foundations of morality.

With this said, however, I do suspect that atheism faces a problem with evil, or perhaps a problem with how to give it its due. What I have in mind is the idea that atheism has a difficult time explaining or accounting for just how horrible some evils strike us as being. It is true that the torture of children or the grotesquely orchestrated sufferings we sometimes hear have been executed by serial killers are morally wrong and can be called as much by naturalistic moral theories. And it is true that world-historical cataclysms like the Lisbon earthquake or the 2004 tsunami can rightly be recognized by the atheist to be bad. But can the sufferings of these events be given by the atheist the radical moral or axiological import we are quite naturally inclined to attribute to them? Here I am not so sure.

What theism supports and atheism must, it seems, reject is a picture of the universe as essentially moral, as having fundamental goodness at its core. If theism is true, then maximal goodness is at the center of all existence. Infinite personal love is the foundation of reality. This is why theism has a chance, at least, of accounting for our experience of some horrors as fundamentally contrary to the way things ought to be – as assault on the essential goodness of the world. Theism can provide a framework within which Miltonian evil (the evil symbolized by Milton's Satan, who chooses to treat evil as good) can be recognized for what it is: a profound perversion of the deepest possible good, a revolt against reality. This is what I do think we feel when we hear of genocide in all of its detail, or when we learn of a child in India who has died of thirst after three horrible days buried beneath the rubble of a building destroyed by an earthquake, all after having seen his mother killed by the initial collapse. It is not just that these things should not have happened, but that their happening is a positive affront to the goodness of the world. It seems to me not enough to say that genocide does not satisfy the hedonic calculus or is irrational in the Kantian sense or is contrary to principles no one could reasonably reject – though, of course, these things are certainly true. Any naturalistically plausible story of what it is for a state of affairs to be bad will render the verdict that the Indian boy's plight was indeed a bad one.

But will that be enough for us? Will it capture our sense of the fundamental unacceptability of these kinds of occurrences? I think not. Because our moral outrage, our axiological revulsion, in the face of such events appears to require the concept of the transgression of essential and complete goodness, atheism is in a bind to account for it. Without the idea of the fundamental moral grain of the universe, an idea quite at home within theism but foreign to atheism, nothing can really be as bad as we ordinarily take some things to be; nothing can be so ultimately *against* the moral grain of the universe as child sex-slavery or the systematic destruction of human personality (effected either by degenerative disease or ingenious torture) strike the vast majority of us as being. Atheism has, therefore, a problem of profound evil. The badness or wrongness that the atheist can ascribe to the most gruesome evils fails to capture its profundity; in the end, then, the evils of a godless world are not really so bad or wrong as theism can declare them to be.

Of course, one way for the atheist to address this problem of profound evil is to accept that nothing really is as bad as our faint hearts imagine, and to argue that the contrary appearance is a function of our hyper-sentimentality – itself, no doubt, the result of the pernicious patronage of theistic religion. This may be right. But making this move is a dangerous gambit for the atheist. Not only will he be in the unenviable position of having to tutor our moral sensibilities out of views that seem to most of us to be quite compelling. He will also have to avoid tutoring us so well that the desiccated remains of moral outrage can no longer motivate us to raise the problem of evil against *theism*. I do not say that the atheist absolutely cannot achieve these goals. I do think, however, that achieving them can be seen to be difficult enough that the problem of profound evil should be taken as a further reason to conclude that the theist is rational to maintain belief in God despite the existence of the world's horrors.

6.2   More To Think About

With my case for the rationality of theistic belief in the face of evil tentatively complete, we can turn now to some reflection on topics we have been forced either to ignore or elide. In this brief book we have been able to review and assess only a subset of the more influential and prominent arguments in the contemporary debate over the problem of evil. We have, alas, neglected countless issues along the way. But perhaps I can limit the damage done through this neglect by being explicit about some of the things I have neglected which are certainly worthy of your further philosophical attention.

Take, for one prominent example, my cavalier use of the term "horrors" and my general failure to say much about the distinguishing features of the most horrible kinds of evil. Marilyn Adams has done very important work on the nature of what she calls "horrendous evils." According to Adams, horrendous evils are ones "the participation in (the doing or suffering of) which gives one reason prima facie to doubt whether one's life could (given their inclusion in it) be a great good to one on the whole" (Adams and Adams 1990, 211). The idea is that some evils a human being can experience, either as victim or victimizer, threaten to undermine the overall goodness of that human life, making it at least appear reasonable to wonder if this particular human being might have been better off never having existed. Adams takes the crushing reality of such horrors to generate a special problem for theism. In fact, she argues that despite the supposed success of Plantinga's Free Will Defense with respect to evil understood in some abstract sense, there remains a forceful logical problem of horrendous evils.

The reason that horrendous evils present a special problem for the coherence of theism, according to Adams, is that she is convinced (plausibly, on my view) that a loving God must be *good* to each creature. That is, a being worthy of the title "God" will have to give to each creature a life that is, overall, a good thing for that creature. Accepting this view of divine goodness places an important constraint on how the theist can conceive of God's justification for permitting the suffering of creatures. On some defenses, it seems as if it would be good enough if God were able to bring it about that the total balance of good over bad in the universe turns out to be pretty high. Yes, some folks may have the misfortune of being stuck with overall bad lives, but this will be balanced off by lots of other goods in other parts of the creation, so that the net goodness is worth the price of the local losses for some individuals. On Adams' view, this will not do, precisely because it would allow that God is able to be (i.e., it is consistent with maximal goodness that God be) less than good to every particular person. The result is that balancing off the evils of the world in a way that leaves some people with overall bad lives is incompatible with the view of divine goodness that Adams commends. But the existence of horrendous evils makes special trouble because these evils, remember, are so disastrous to the people who are caught in them that we find ourselves suspecting that they would have been better off had they not been brought into existence at all. What Adams attempts to do, then, is show how it is *possible* that, despite the reality of horrendous evils, God is good to everyone – even to those who suffer the horrors (1990). (Contrary to Adams' claims on this point, for what it is worth, I do not think that her concerns amount to a reason to deny that the free will defense has succeeded. This is because, as you will recall, the logical problem must be framed by considerations that the atheologian can plausibly insist are either essential to theism or are necessary truths; and the atheologian cannot, by my lights, plausibly insist that the deep moral and theological commitments that shape Adams' concerns are either necessary or essential in the relevant ways. Now, I am, as I have suggested, inclined to accept her moral and theological commitments myself. So I am grateful for her efforts to show how God can continue to be good to those who suffer horrors under these conditions. Indeed, I have included her treatment of horrendous evil in this section [on topics that I believe have been under-treated in this book] precisely because of the deep insight into the wider problem of evil for theism that it reveals. Including Adams' treatment of horrors here, and for this reason, is, I hope, compatible with rejecting her own motivations for addressing the problem and with not including it in chapter 2's response to the logical problem – where I would have been forced to render a negative verdict.)

Another topic we have essentially ignored has to do with the fact that a great many of the world's evils are distinctively social and structural. Ted Poston has given some precision to the idea of "social evil" by reflecting on the way evil and suffering can ramify in complex decision situations. A social evil is a bad outcome the badness of which cannot be reduced to the badness constituted or caused directly by individual choices. When the overall badness is, as it were, out of proportion to the badness (if any) contributed by each individual decision, there is a new species of evil that needs to be explained and, presumably, accommodated by theism. Poston notes that many evils of the modern world are social in this way. His paradigm case involves a water shortage in California.

> Suppose you are a resident of Los Angeles and the greater Los Angeles area is facing a serious water shortage. The reservoirs in northern California are running dry; the Los Angeles and San Gabriel rivers are bone dry; even Oregon's plentiful lakes and rivers are ominously diminished. Without a significant decrease in overall water consumption, the Los Angeles area will run out of an adequate water supply. City planners foresee the possibility of severely restricting residential water use. If most residents significantly decrease their water consumption – by not watering lawns, washing cars, or letting the tap run unnecessarily – the Los Angeles area will manage until the winter rains come. Obviously, it is in the best interest of all that most everyone follows this advice. But this represents a considerable cost to each person. If, for example, you decrease your water usage, your carefully cultivated garden and fruit trees will wilt and die. This is a hefty burden to pay. However, if no one decreases his water usage, each will pay an even greater cost. Yet you realize that if most everyone decreases his water consumption, then you may continue your normal usage without any ill consequence. Moreover, because the benefit of decreased water usage requires a very large number of participants – well over a million homeowners – your own individual contribution does not affect whether or not the benefit is realized. (2014, 3)

Now, if an insufficient number of Angelenos restrict their water usage and a serious drought results, we have an instance of a social evil. Notice that the exorbitant evil that will be constituted and caused by this drought cannot be thought of as the simple sum of the badness of each particular person's decision not to comply with the water restriction demands. This is because no single person's failure to comply makes so much as the tiniest causal contribution to the terrible result. Holding everything else fixed, the single person's compliance would have made absolutely no difference to the outcome. Some will see that social evil, understood in Poston's terms, bears a striking resemblance to the "tragedies of the commons" that Garrett Hardin has infamously brought to prominent contemporary attention (1968).

The unique challenge presented by social evils, according to Poston, is that it is hard to see how the traditional theodic responses are going to be able to help explain why God would permit them. Social evils are not, strictly speaking, moral evils, because they do not depend on the free choices of a *single* individual. If this is right, the kind of appeal to free will that we have seen in both the free will defense and in free will theodicies will seem to have no foothold for dealing with this kind of social evil. At the same time, however, it isn't appropriate to characterize social evil as a species of natural evil, either. This is because these social evils do, unlike standard forms of natural evil, result from the free choices of creatures (albeit, from the complex interactions of their free choices, but from their free choices nonetheless) and not merely from the ordinary interaction of matter in accord with the laws of nature. Notice, however, that the typical strategies of response to natural evil that we have canvassed (the appeal to the values of stable laws and of soul-making, for example) also look powerless to deal with distinctively social evil. It may be, then, that the theist will have to go further than she has so far to provide either a theodicy or a defense for this kind of evil.

I have also been far too brief in addressing the evil of animal suffering, though we have not neglected it completely, having had various occasions at least to mention it along the way. Still, it would be a grave mistake to give the impression that matters are in any way settled about just how serious the problem of animal suffering is or about how theism can reasonably respond to it (cf. Murray 2011). A similar short-ness of shrift has been given to various strands of theodicy beyond those invoking free will, soul-making, and the value of the laws of nature. We have ignored, for example, Richard Swinburne's striking claims about the value of being of use, which have provoked no small response from critics. Additional values, like the value of being able to appreciate goodness or the value of building special kinds of connections among God's creatures, have also been deployed in contemporary efforts at theodicy (cf. McBrayer and Howard-Snyder 2013). And Marilyn Adams has made the intriguing claim that theodicy need not function by being explanatory at all (as my presentation has presumed). That is, she claims that a theodicy can proceed not by providing supposedly morally sufficient reasons God may have for allowing evil, but by demonstrating how God can be good to each creature even while permitting the world's evils.

Each of these elements of the contemporary debate has been treated either too quickly or not at all throughout this book; though I have been able only briefly to mention them here, I submit that these aspects of the contemporary discussion will repay careful attention and, in fact, promise (in my assessment) to be the contexts for fruitful new discussion.

6.3   Common Theism Alone?

Some final thoughts about restricting ourselves to consideration of the problems of evil in terms of bare or (as I've been calling it) common theism are in order. The principal idea from the beginning has been to try to reflect on the challenge evil presents for theism *simpliciter*, leaving aside any special challenges that evil might present for particular versions of theism – Christian theism, Jewish theism, Islamic theism, etc. From the point of view of our central goal of understanding the main contours of the contemporary debate, this has been a perfectly sensible strategy. Abstracting away from the specific doctrinal or theological commitments of particular theistic worldviews has certainly helped us to stay focused on those aspects of evil that make trouble for all forms of theistic belief as such. I would not, however, want to leave you with the impression that there is something intrinsically philosophically valuable about restricting our reflection in this way. In fact, there may be some reason to think that the restriction can dangerously impede our deepest understanding of matters in this domain. At the very least, I want to encourage you not to feel any philosophical pressure to impose this restriction on your ongoing exploration of the problem of evil.

One additional practical motivation for limiting myself to common theism has been, frankly, that I know so little about theistic traditions outside Christianity. At the same time, as I have mentioned, distinctively *Christian* theism has been the principal foil for contemporary analytic philosophy of religion (and for treatment of the problems of evil especially). This may be a purely sociological phenomenon. In any case, I propose to loosen this restriction for these brief concluding moments and consider the challenge of evil for Christianity in particular. Why? Well, as it turns out, I take myself to know enough about Christian philosophical theology not to embarrass myself with a display of transparent ignorance. Also, since the current debate has been preoccupied by Christian theism, these concluding points promise to give you even deeper insight into the contemporary philosophical discussion of the problem of evil. But most importantly, I am hoping that these specifically Christian reflections can function as paradigms or templates that might be filled in in decidedly Jewish or Islamic ways by those who know more about those traditions.[1]

A natural point of entry is the renewed recognition among Christian philosophers that the details of Christianity may indeed matter both for how the problem of evil is framed and for what resources can be brought to bear in response to it. This thought has been perhaps slower in emerging among contemporary philosophers of religion than might have been expected. Still, it is emerging and, to my mind, bearing considerable fruit. Take Richard Swinburne's admission:

> I had assumed [in an earlier book] that theodicy does not need to bring in doctrines peculiar to different religions (such as reincarnation in eastern religions; or life after death in a new world etc. in Christianity), in order to show that the occurrence of evil does not count against the existence of God. I

am not fully convinced of that anymore. In any case most contemporary humans are a lot more likely to be convinced if theodicy does bring in such doctrines. (1998, xi)

With respect to the special resources of Christianity for facing the problem of evil, I will highlight a pair of recent developments. First, consider Marilyn Adams' Christological appeal. According to Christianity, God has entered into the world, in the person of Jesus of Nazareth, in a stunning way; God has become a particular human being. This doctrine of the incarnation of the second person of the Trinity, Adams claims, allows the Christian thinker to appropriate a very distinctive form of identificationism to account for how even grotesque suffering can be made sufficiently meaningful so as not to undermine the overall value of the life of the sufferer. At the crucifixion, the Christian philosopher can emphasize, God (God!) suffered a horrendous evil. At the resurrection, the horror of this evil is seen not to be the end of the story. Indeed, the resurrection is a promise of the final consummation of all things and of God's ability, on account of unlimited divine resourcefulness, to bring all things together in the complete joy of the beatific vision. This means that the one who suffers a horror will eventually be able to see that her suffering has put her in a unique position to be deeply related, *via* identification, to the God who has suffered. "Hence," she concludes, "God's identification with human participation in horrors enables God to defeat their evil aspect within the course of the individual participant's life" (1999, 167).[2]

Another recent and important appropriation of the resources of Christianity in response to the problem of evil is due to Eleonore Stump (2012) who draws expressly on biblical stories to fill out a detailed defense. (She emphasizes the defensive tenor of her broadly Thomistic approach to the problem of suffering, but also notes that her argument will constitute a theodicy for anyone who is inclined to think that the premises of her argument are not just possibly true but quite plausibly true.) Her strategy is to paint a vivid picture of a world overseen by God that also contains suffering of the sort we encounter. Since the goal of a defense is to show that the world's evils are in some sense compatible with the existence of God, a well-painted picture of the kind Stump attempts can amount to (or be an essential component of) a forceful defense. Stump's narrative palette is taken specifically from the biblical accounts of Job, Samson, Abraham, and Mary of Bethany. By exploring these narratives and the distinctively second-personal encounters with God that each central character experiences in the midst of his or her suffering, Stump takes herself to show that God can enter into and comfort human beings in their suffering without diminishing or minimizing it. This thought can, she goes on to argue, contribute to a distinctively Christian defense (and perhaps even a theodicy) in the spirit of Thomas Aquinas. Crucially, Stump emphasizes that the biblical narratives need not be taken to describe actual events revealed to us by God in order for the defense to succeed – remember, once again, that a defense needs only premises that are true for all we know rather than premises we have good reason to accept. Still, it should be clear just how much Stump's approach proceeds not on the basis of merely common theism but by appealing to the fuller resources of Christian Scripture and the history and theology of Christian biblical interpretation.

My principal reason for very briefly exploring the possibility of distinctively Christian resources for facing the problems of evil is, I reiterate, to counteract any impression I may have given that approaching the problems of this book from the standpoint of common theism is the only or best way to go. This strikes me as far from the truth; and, indeed, the particular efforts that Marilyn Adams and Eleonore Stump (among others I have been forced to ignore) have made to appropriate robust Christian theology into theistic responses to evil appear to me to be among the most promising and fruitful. In addition, I can see no reason why Jewish and Islamic thinkers would be unable to make similar theologically invested efforts to deal with evil as it arises for and within their particular traditions.

6.4   The End and the Beginning

I hope you will excuse the naïveté of my hope that you will now go forward with both the knowledge and motivation to make your own contributions to the contemporary debate regarding the problem of evil. And maybe you will tolerate this much naïveté if I add that I do not expect you to accept my governing judgment about the rationality of theistic belief in the light of evil (though I would be thrilled if you would). I am, alas, not quite *that* naïve. Philosophy – and this set of issues within philosophy especially – is too hard and too deep for it to be even minimally reasonable to hope that any conclusion as pointed as the one I have defended could win general acceptance.

Remember, too, however, that I have been at pains to make sure that you see just how weak the claim I have been defending turns out to be. I claim that there are some people, some theists, who despite competent awareness of the strongest versions of arguments for atheism from evil are still rational in maintaining their theistic commitments. Even if this is right, it doesn't tell us much about the rationality of the wider parties interested in this debate. For example, should the atheist stick to her atheism in response to the arguments offered here? I haven't argued to the contrary. Perhaps she should. Perhaps she shouldn't. Should the agnostic be swayed in the direction of theism by these arguments? I haven't attempted to insist that this is so. Perhaps he should. Perhaps he shouldn't. Are all theists rational in their theistic beliefs? I certainly haven't claimed anything even nearly this strong, and it strikes me as at least *prima facie* implausible that they would be – but the arguments I have offered here say very little about this. Maybe, then, even if I have not persuaded you that theism enjoys the rationality I claim it does, I will venture to hope that you can now see that the claim, when distinguished from claims with which it might be confused, is not completely indefensible.

In this spirit, I will conclude by recognizing one final time that Ivan Karamazov strikes a profound pose and casts a long shadow over the problem of evil in the contemporary world. There is something brave indeed, and even inspiring, in the image of this icon of modernity standing before the supposed God, gesticulating with his faux ticket and pretending to throw it down in his refusal to enter into the religious game. To register an essentially moral complaint against the author of our moral existence is to be heroic in a distinctively modern way. Dostoevsky knew this, of course, and crafted the image precisely to give this kind of heroism its proper respect. But another kind of heroism can also get a foothold in our psyches – one marked not so much by resistance as by humility and even (gods forbid) submission. Alyosha Karamazov, Father Zossima, and the ridiculous man are given to us by Dostoevsky as heroes of this second kind (and their real-world counterparts are, obviously enough, to be found in the Assisis, Calcuttas, and Birmingham jails where prayer and preaching are wedded to concrete justice).

We can all agree that our encounters with evil, our inevitable suffering, will call for heroism. Of which kind? I submit to you that the fact of evil itself, even in all of its full-blooded reality, does not force you to accept Ivan's.

Notes

Chapter 1

1 Thanks to Lori Speak for the terminology of "common theism."
2 This raises a good question about whether God, if such a being exists, has a name. According to the Judeo-Christian tradition, God may indeed have a name or at least be willing to be addressed in terms of one. Moses is famously encouraged by God to use the name "Yahweh," roughly translated as "I am who I am." Tantalizing as the philosophical implications of this name are, I will set them aside.
3 I saw them at work in Joshua's tragic case as well. In response to Joshua's death, his father essentially abandoned the religious commitments he had previously cultivated. By contrast Joshua's mother Mary found some solace in her faith and what she took to be its explanatory power.
4 It does seem, however, that Dostoevsky had hoped to answer Ivan's challenge in *The Brothers Karamazov* – by way of narrating the life of the saintly Elder Zossima. In fact, Dostoevsky appears to have worried that Ivan's case had come off a bit more forcefully than had the response he offers to it in the person of Zossima. For some effort to make Dostoevsky's thinking here philosophically rigorous, see Timothy O'Connor (2009).
5 The unusual counter-instance is when someone's personal suffering is partly a result of their facing the conceptual tensions of one or more of the philosophical problems. These cases are rare but not non-existent. My sensitive student's case may have

been one of these. Dealing with them is a very delicate matter. Disentangling the personal from the philosophical aspects of the problem in such cases requires sensitivity and patience.
6   Alvin Plantinga expresses similar sentiments about the limits of philosophical arguments in this domain. See Plantinga (1974, 28–9).

Chapter 2

1   It might be argued that Hume's explanatory structure and tone is a concession to his still predominantly religious culture and his interest in not upsetting the establishment with transparently atheistic arguments. Maybe so. But this gives us another account of the distinctively "contemporary" nature of Mackie's article: in it, he feels no need to soften its atheistic force either for editors or for his would-be readership.
2   You don't know about the Chupacabra? Check it out: http://en.wikipedia.org/wiki/Chupacabra
3   The logical problem of evil is also frequently called the "deductive problem of evil" because the atheistic conclusion is supposed to be deducible from the propositions accepted by the theist.
4   Others who appear to take up Mackie's torch for logical inconsistency in theistic commitments include Flew (1955), Aiken (1957), and McCloskey (1960).
5   In an early version of his free will defense, Plantinga is rather charitable to Mackie on this point. He allows that "Mackie's second additional premise, if a bit imprecise, is on the whole unexceptionable," but goes on to add that, "[i]t needs a small qualification that Mackie himself no doubt intended; what we must say is that there are no *nonlogical* limits to what an omnipotent being can do" (1967, 118–19). That Mackie intended this sensible qualification without prejudice is not at all clear to me. Mackie does go on to say, at a later point in the essay, that the view of omnipotence as constrained by logic "may, indeed, be accepted as a modification of our original account which does not reject anything that is essential to theism, and I shall in general assume it in subsequent discussion" (1955, 28). I am not convinced, however, that Mackie is doing anything other than attempting to get some rhetorical mileage out of this apparent concession. If Mackie had intended the qualification from the beginning, and had no intentions of treating its invocation as a kind of weakening of

the commonsensically motivated view, then there is no especially good account of why he waits until this later point to add it. At the very least, Plantinga's suggestion that Mackie all along *meant* to include this qualification (simply forgetting about it, perhaps, or thinking it so obvious as to need no expression?) when formulating his quasi-logical rules strikes me now as somewhat too charitable.

6 Alas, of course, there are some dissenters who believe that Plantinga's defense does not succeed. See DeRose (1991) and Howard-Snyder and O'Leary-Hawthorne (1998). We will take up some of their concerns in the closing sections of this chapter. Also, Marilyn McCord Adams has complained that Plantinga's defense solves only the *abstract* logical problem but leaves the *concrete* logical problem largely untouched (1999). I will say a little more about this in chapter 6.

7 Here I am following DeRose (1991).

8 And, of course, any propositions entailed by these.

9 For Plantinga's reasoning on this point, see (1967, 118).

10 In God's case, the bracketed bit can be ignored – because of omniscience.

11 To get the strict entailment, we might have to add a clause to the effect that the highest goods made possible by free will outweigh (or defeat or are justifiably worth the risk of permitting) the evils contingent upon free will. But building this into (C) makes it even more unwieldy than it already is.

12 Plantinga also quotes this section of Mackie's article (see Adams and Adams 1990, 86).

13 Descartes famously appears to have thought otherwise; but he is most definitely the minority report in the history of philosophy. The standard view is that these kinds of abstract objects and logical truths are uncreated features of reality; they do not, however, exist independently of God – nothing can pull off independence from God, on this traditional view. Rather, they depend on God even while being uncreated. Thus, God is *logically* and *explanatorily*, even if not *temporally*, prior to them.

14 I am eliding a great deal of controversial philosophical theology here. Plantinga is, in essence, assuming (or re-inventing) the view of divine knowledge and providence now known as "Molinism" – named after the medieval Jesuit thinker Luis de Molina, who formulated a powerful version of this view. According to Molinism, God knows not just all the necessary truths (how things have to be) and all the contingent truths (how things are), but also all of the counterfactual/conditional truths (how things could have been). God, therefore, has "middle knowledge" – knowledge of truths that are "between"

the necessary and the contingent – which applies even to genuinely free choices. This means that God knows what every free being *would do* in whatever circumstances each could be placed. This is what makes it sensible to imagine, as I do in the text, that God is able to "see" all the possible worlds even before actualizing one of them. The canonical contemporary statement and defense of Molinism is Flint (1998). For immersion into ongoing controversies regarding this view, see Perszyk (2011).

15 A recent survey of professional philosophers returned results according to which nearly sixty percent leaned toward compatibilism, while less than thirty percent (and perhaps considerably fewer) favored incompatibilism. See the Philpapers survey results at: http://philpapers.org/surveys/results.pl

16 For some of these developments, see Fischer and Ravizza (1998), Watson (2004), and Nelkin (2012), among many others.

17 According to agent-causalism, a free action is one that is caused directly by the agent as a substance and not by, for example, events internal to the agent. For some details and explanation, see Clarke and Capes (2013).

18 This is not to say that I agree with their skepticism. Indeed, I do not. My point is that even if one does accept the most skeptical contemporary views, the free will defense is not challenged.

19 Furthermore, as I read Clarke's argument, it depends crucially on his complaints about the possibility, in general, of substance causation. Theists, I believe, should not be especially impressed with this argument since it turns on considerations that would seem to make it impossible for God to be the cause of the universe.

20 I leave for homework the task of formalizing the incompatibility of the two modal claims. Also, I should add that I am eliding considerable (and intriguing) argumentative detail in this brief treatment of Howard-Snyder and Hawthorne's article.

21 Plantinga himself is not persuaded. See his objections in (2009). For Howard-Snyder's replies, see his (2013).

22 In a recent paper (2012), Alexander Pruss purports to show that universal transworld depravity is impossible. The argument is complex and rests on what Pruss himself admits is a "controversial counterfactual Dominance Principle." Indeed, I think there are good reasons, that I won't go into here, to reject this principle. Furthermore, this argument presupposes (as does Plantinga's original defense) that Molinism is true. But

Molinism appears to be neither necessarily true nor an essential commitment of theism, whatever its vocal proponents may have to say about it. The theist, then, need not accept it in responding to the logical problem of evil. As I will emphasize in closing this chapter, I follow Plantinga himself in thinking that it is even easier for the free will defense to succeed if we give up Molinism – a move, on my view, that is independently motivated.

23 That is, Plantinga assumed that God has the "middle knowledge" associated with Molinism. See note 14 above. At least, I am convinced he made it harder on himself. For doubts about this, see Perszyk (1998).

24 Would this mean that God is not omniscient? I don't think so. Suppose that omniscience is a matter of knowing the truth-value of every proposition that has a truth-value. Propositions about what free beings will do in future with their freedom may have, I suggest, no determinate truth-value. That God does not know the truth-value of propositions that lack one would not bring omniscience into question – anymore than God's inability to work logical contradictions brings divine omnipotence into question. This view is a crucial plank in the position known as "Open Theism." For an exploration and defense of this view, see Hasker (1989, especially chapter 10).

Chapter 3

1 For a detailed treatment of Rowe's development of the evidential problem, see Trakakis (2007).

2 The unfortunate sufferers in these cases are sometimes referred to as "Bambi" and "Sue" respectively, following Alston (1996).

3 Keep in mind that if what it costs to avoid the intense suffering is *not* worse than the intense suffering, then there *is* an overriding reason to permit the suffering: namely, avoiding the cost.

4 During the writing of this chapter alone, we had tragic news of, for example, a factory collapse in Bangladesh that killed more than 1,100 people and of a tornado that tore through an Oklahoma City suburb, taking deadly aim at an elementary school in its last week of classes before summer break.

5 Must the skeptical theist at least have some compelling *evidence* for theism in order to launch her response (as Frances [2013] seems to suggest)? I don't think so. Perhaps it is true that she will need to have some *warrant* for her theism. But this warrant need not come by way of evidence; theistic belief

may, after all, turn out to be properly basic. See Plantinga (2000).

6   Some confusion about this point has been cleared up in the philosophical debate. Initially, Wykstra took up the project of showing that there are good reasons to think that a principle like (GOODS) is false (see his 1996, 137 for his confessions to this effect). And, in fact, I am inclined to think that he was right that there are such good reasons. However, efforts to resist Wykstra's arguments were not without force. These efforts took advantage, however, of Wykstra's boldness, showing, we might say, that he had not made a decisive case for the falsity of (GOODS). After repenting of his youthful boldness, Wykstra now emphasizes that the opponent of Rowe's argument needs only to show that (GOODS) has enough against it to justify us in withholding judgment regarding its truth.

7   There is a further ambiguity to which we may need to attend. Suppose God has a good reason for permitting evils of a certain kind, but it is an arbitrary matter (perhaps a matter of chance) which particular instances of this kind are allowed to occur. Will these allowed instances count as gratuitous in the sense relevant to Rowe's argument? For example, suppose God is going to have to allow one or the other of two innocent people to drown. Assume that there are very good reasons such that God cannot save them both. But also assume, now, that God has no good reasons to prefer the saving of one over the other. In such a case, will the drowning God permits here count as gratuitous? I think it should not. It is true, surely enough, that God has no good reason for permitting *this* drowning rather than *that* drowning; but God still retains a good reason (we are supposing) for permitting some drowning or other. This would seem to me to be enough to conclude that the actual drowning is not gratuitous.

8   If the proponent of Rowe's argument opts for an account of gratuitousness in terms of GE2, then it is considerably more difficult to see how the theological premise could be false. However, it is also even more difficult to see why we should accept Rowe's argument that the empirical premise is true.

9   For details regarding Open Theism, see Pinnock et al. (1994) and Rhoda (2008).

10   Keep in mind that nothing I am saying here entails or is even meant to suggest that we (or God) should blame the sufferers for their free response to the leukemia or that the sufferers should have responded differently. The point is only that God may have reasonably counted on a different free response – one

that would have involved the existence of sufficiently justifying goods – that did not obtain.

11 Might it be replied that it is the good of robust free will that is providing the sufficient justification for God's permission of the suffering? And, then, won't it turn out that the suffering is not gratuitous after all? I'm not sure; but I am tempted to say no. It is true that it is the good of robust free will that justifies God in permitting the *possibility* that someone will suffer gratuitously. But does this entail that the suffering is not gratuitous? It seems to me not. In fact, it might be argued that the possibility of someone's suffering gratuitously is precisely the price of serious freedom. To eliminate this real possibility would be to eliminate the seriousness of the freedom.

12 Peter van Inwagen has offered a related objection to the theological premise according to which TP assumes that there is some minimum amount of evil God must permit in order to achieve greater goods. However, van Inwagen argues that the minimum claim should not be accepted; and, therefore, neither should the theological premise that presupposes it. See his (1988) and (1991). For discussion, see Howard-Snyder and Howard-Snyder (1999).

13 For what it is worth, I think that the advantages of accepting Open Theism do ultimately outweigh the disadvantages. But for concerns with the disadvantages here, see Trakakis (2005, section 2.b).

14 For a more detailed response along these lines in defense of skeptical theism, see Bergmann (2001), especially section II.C.

15 For more on this, see Rea (2013).

16 Rowe's argument is only one of a few evidential arguments that purport to support atheism. Here it is at least worth mentioning Paul Draper's influential version of the evidential argument, even though we don't have space to treat it in any detail (see Draper 1989). Taking his cue from David Hume, Draper takes an indirect approach. While Rowe argues directly from the existence of supposedly gratuitous evils to the non-existence of God, Draper attempts to argue that the existence of the evils we find is better explained by another thesis, what he calls the Hypothesis of Indifference (or HI), a thesis that is inconsistent with theism. According to HI, the conditions of the beings capable of suffering are simply not the result of any supernatural entity. The universe has no particular agenda with respect to how pain and pleasure are distributed throughout it; in short, the universe is indifferent to suffering. Draper claims that HI is much more likely than theism to be true. That is, the probability that HI is true, given what we know about

how pain and pleasure occur in our world, is much higher than the probability that theism is true. In particular, Draper emphasizes that if theism is true, then we should expect the pains and pleasures of our world to be much more tightly associated with merit than they turn out to be. The fact that most suffering looks to have nothing to do with desert is to be expected on the hypothesis of indifference; by contrast, this fact should be surprising if God exists. Therefore, the wide and apparently arbitrary distribution of undeserved suffering throughout the sentient universe should be taken as strong inductive evidence in favor of HI over theism. And, since HI is inconsistent with theism, it should therefore be taken as strong inductive evidence that theism is false. For a response in the spirit of Skeptical Theism, see van Inwagen (1991).

Chapter 4

1   I say *almost* everyone because there are at least two fairly small groups of people who would falsify the unrestricted generalization. Some people have no interest whatsoever in discovering that God exists. The now-standard case in point is Thomas Nagel, who famously explained: "It isn't just that I don't believe in God and, naturally, hope that I'm right in my belief. It's that I hope there is no God! I don't want there to be a God; I don't want the universe to be like that" (1997, 130). The second group would include those few individuals who, for whatever reason, are already supremely confident that God exists. Thus, the members of the first group do not want more confidence and the members of the second purport not to need it. I detect some irrationality in both groups, but won't here attempt to draw it out rigorously.
2   There will be more to say explicitly about Rowe's concern with the parent analogy in section 4.6.
3   I have subtracted some description and added the bracketed bits and the "therefores" in premises (4) and (5) in order to simplify the presentation.
4   In later work (for example, Schellenberg 2005a), Schellenberg modally strengthens premise (2), raising it to the level of a conceptual truth. We can ignore this strengthening for our purposes.
5   It may be interesting to note, however, that despite Schellenberg's insistence that the argument has a decidedly evidential form, he nevertheless insists that it supports atheism and *not*

agnosticism. This is because the reasonability of agnosticism is, in effect, the evidence under consideration. If agnosticism is reasonable, Schellenberg argues, then atheism is likely. So the considerations to which the argument appeals can seem to rule out agnosticism as a reasonable response to the evidence. For debate on this point, see Draper (2001) and Schellenberg's reply (2005a).

6   I leave aside the question of whether Paul *intended* his statements as an account of all theistic nonbelief.

7   Pascal makes a point along these lines: "Wishing to appear openly to those who seek him whole-heartedly, and to remain hidden from those who single-mindedly avoid him, God qualified the way he might be known so that he gave visible signs to those who seek him, and none to those who do not. There is enough light for those whose only desire is to see, and enough darkness for those of the opposite disposition" (1995, 81).

8   There may be *some* people who would be robbed of one or another of the important goods by having reasonable unbelief made impossible for them (see Murray 2001). If so, then the existence of these people may be enough to give the theist a very thin defense of her rejection of premise (2). Still, it would remain implausible for the theist to insist that all reasonable nonbelief could be accounted for in terms of God's efforts to preserve these goods for this smallish group of people.

9   Replies along these lines probably also presuppose that something like Molinism is true and that God has "middle knowledge." To the degree that you are skeptical about the possibility of such knowledge (as I am), you will also be skeptical about this effort to challenge premise (2).

10   McBrayer and Swenson (2012) do an especially nice job of motivating and challenging this defense, which they call the "Improper Response Defense."

11   I ignore, for considerations of space, a cumulative attack on premise (2). Such an attack would proceed by combining the range of goods God might be aiming to secure and evils God might be aiming to avoid into a fuller explanation of the existence of reasonable nonbelief. In other words, it may be that no single good or evil can account for all reasonable nonbelief but that, nevertheless, a multiplicity of them, properly ordered, can do the trick. Schellenberg considers and rejects this type of strategy with surprising quickness (see 1993, 205–7). For some of the resources that might be deployed in a defense of this sort, see sections 2.4 and 2.5 of the introduction to Howard-Snyder and Moser (2001).

12 However, see note 11 again for the possibility of a defense that deploys all (and perhaps more) of these reasons in a cumulative case against premise (2).

13 Notice that (B) is equivalent to (or at least entails) premise (2) of Schellenberg's argument.

14 See McBrayer and Swenson (2012) for development of this point.

15 For further defense of skeptical theism, see chapter 3, especially sections 3.3 and 3.6.

16 I think the thought experiment works even if we suppose that the evidence sufficiently supports my continuing belief that Lori is, in fact, dead; but let's ignore this stronger position.

17 Poston and Dougherty (2007) consider similar cases in order to make similar points.

18 For an expression of this kind of concern, see Rowe (2001, 156–7).

19 For a brief effort at some of this additional philosophical work, see Bergmann (2009).

Chapter 5

1 Some philosophers keep "theodicy" as the term for the general project and then distinguish defensive theodicies from explanatory theodicies as species within the wider genus.

2 The two most fully developed (and widely discussed) contemporary theodicies are those of Hick (1978) and Swinburne (1998).

3 See Clarke (2003) for a careful presentation and defense of these arguments.

4 See my (2013) for complaints about both Hick and Swinburne in this regard. Swinburne has since published *Mind, Brain, and Free Will* (2013) in which he takes some steps toward discharging the duty to defend libertarianism. I leave it to the reader to assess the strength of Swinburne's case.

5 Hick's talk of "souls" and "soul-making" doesn't commit him to any particular ontology of the human person, as far as I can tell. What he appears to mean by the "soul" is something like the moral core or character of a person; that which is changed and fortified by moral and spiritual formation. Parenthetically, Hick credits the poet John Keats with the phrase "vale of soul-making" (1978, 295 n. 1).

6 To his credit, Hick recognizes this category of suffering, helpfully characterizes it as "dysteleological," and makes some

effort to address the problems it creates for his theodicy. For his response to dysteleological suffering, see especially (1978, 334).

7   For even more contemporary efforts at theodicy, see McBrayer and Howard-Snyder (2013).

8   The appearance of conflict between the approaches taken by Plantinga and Swinburne respectively is somewhat eased by Swinburne's admission, in a footnote to his (1998), that his own concept of theodicy "is much closer to what Plantinga calls a 'defence'" (15 n. 8). The tension, however, is not completely removed, because Swinburne's theodicy, while indeed closer to it, is still more demanding than a Plantinga-style defense.

9   This is in keeping with his commitment to epistemic internalism. I extract these conditions for success from Swinburne (1998, 14–16).

10 van Inwagen himself thinks that no argument for any substantive philosophical positions can be a success on these conditions.

11 For permission to use portions of my (2013) in this chapter, I would like to thank John Wiley & Sons and the editors of the volume in which it appears, Justin McBrayer and Daniel Howard-Snyder.

Chapter 6

1   We shouldn't ignore that there are much more fine-grained distinctions between and within theistic traditions than my presentation in the text might suggest. Roman Catholic Christianity may face the problem of evil in a different way than does, say, Dutch Reformed Christianity (and both may have distinctive resources for addressing the problem). The point I want to emphasize is that the specifics of the tradition are likely to matter and it would therefore be a mistake for philosophers of religion to ignore these specifics.

2   Alvin Plantinga has taken this point somewhat further (far further than Adams would wish to take it, I imagine) to suggest an incarnational theodicy. In his "Supralapsarianism, or 'O Felix Culpa'" (Plantinga 2004), Plantinga attempts to argue that any world with incarnational redemption is better than any world without it. So, sinfulness and its consequences may be necessary for the great good of Christian atonement.

Bibliography

Adams, Marilyn McCord. 1993. "The Problem of Hell: A Problem of Evil for Christians." In *Reasoned Faith*, ed. Eleonore Stump, 301–27. Ithaca, NY: Cornell University Press.

Adams, Marilyn McCord. 1999. *Horrendous Evils and the Goodness of God*. Ithaca, NY: Cornell University Press.

Adams, Marilyn McCord and Robert Merrihew Adams, eds. 1990. *The Problem of Evil*. New York: Oxford University Press.

Adams, Robert Merrihew. 1985. "Plantinga on the Problem of Evil." In *Alvin Plantinga*, ed. Peter van Inwagen and James E. Tomberlin, 225–55. Dordrecht: Reidel.

Aiken, Henry. 1957. "God and Evil." *Ethics* 68: 77–97.

Almeida, Michael and Graham Oppy. 2003. "Sceptical Theism and Evidential Arguments from Evil." *Australasian Journal of Philosophy* 81/4: 496–516.

Alston, William P. 1996. "The Inductive Argument from Evil and the Human Cognitive Condition." In *The Evidential Argument from Evil*, ed. Daniel Howard-Snyder, 97–174. Bloomington, IN: Indiana University Press.

Bergmann, Michael. 2001. "Skeptical Theism and Rowe's New Evidential Argument from Evil." *Nous* 35: 278–96.

Bergmann, Michael. 2009. "Skeptical Theism and the Problem of Evil." In *The Oxford Handbook of Philosophical Theology*, ed. Thomas Flint and Michael Rea, 374–99. Oxford: Oxford University Press.

Byrne, Peter. 2007. "Moral Arguments for God's Existence." In *The Stanford Encyclopedia of Philosophy* (Spring 2013 Edition), ed. Edward N. Zalta. http://plato.stanford.edu/entries/moral-arguments-god/ [accessed 04/03/2014].

Clarke, Randolph. 2003. *Libertarian Accounts of Free Will*. New York: Oxford University Press.

Clarke, Randolph and Justin Capes. 2013. "Incompatibilist (Nondeterministic) Theories of Free Will." In *The Stanford Encyclopedia of Philosophy* (Spring 2013 Edition), ed. Edward N. Zalta. http://plato.stanford.edu/archives/spr2013/entries/incompatibilism-theories/ [accessed 04/03/2014].

Dennett, Daniel. 1984. *Elbow Room: The Varieties of Free Will Worth Wanting*. Cambridge, MA: The MIT Press.

DeRose, Keith. 1991. "Plantinga, Presumption, Possibility, and the Problem of Evil." *Canadian Journal of Philosophy* 21: 497–512.

Dostoevsky, Fyodor. 1877. "The Dream of a Ridiculous Man." Trans. Constance Garnett. http://www.online-literature.com/dostoevsky/3368/ [accessed 04/03/2014].

Dostoevsky, Fyodor. 1982. *The Brothers Karamazov*. New York: Penguin Classics.

Draper, Paul. 1989. "Pain and Pleasure: An Evidential Problem for Theists." *Nous* 23/3: 331–50.

Draper, Paul. 2001. "Seeking But Not Believing: Confessions of a Practicing Agnostic." In *Divine Hiddenness: New Essays*, ed. Daniel Howard-Snyder and Paul Moser, 197–214. New York: Cambridge University Press.

Fischer, John Martin and Mark Ravizza, S. J. 1998. *Responsibility and Control: A Theory of Moral Responsibility*. New York: Cambridge University Press.

Flew, Antony. 1955. "Divine Omnipotence and Human Freedom." In *New Essays in Philosophical Theology*, ed. Antony Flew and Alasdair MacIntyre, 144–69. New York: Macmillan.

Flint, Thomas. 1998. *Divine Providence: The Molinist Account*. Ithaca, NY: Cornell University Press.

Frances, Bryan. 2013. *Gratuitous Suffering and the Problem of Evil: A Comprehensive Introduction*. New York: Routledge.

Gale, Richard. 1996. "Some Difficulties in Theistic Treatments of Evil." In *The Evidential Argument from Evil*, ed. Daniel Howard-Snyder, 206–18. Bloomington, IN: Indiana University Press.

Hardin, Garrett. 1968. "The Tragedy of the Commons." *Science*, New Series, 162/3859: 1243–8.

Hasker, William. 1989. *God, Time, and Knowledge*. Ithaca, NY: Cornell University Press.

Hick, John. 1978. *Evil and the God of Love*, 2nd edn. San Francisco, CA: Harper & Row.

Howard-Snyder, Daniel, ed. 1996. *The Evidential Argument from Evil*. Bloomington, IN: Indiana University Press.

Howard-Snyder, Daniel. 2013. "The Logical Problem of Evil: Mackie and Plantinga." In *The Blackwell Companion to the*

142 *Bibliography*

Problem of Evil, ed. Justin P. McBrayer and Daniel Howard-Snyder, 19–33. Chichester: Wiley-Blackwell.

Howard-Snyder, Daniel and Frances Howard-Snyder. 1999. "Is Theism Compatible with Gratuitous Evil?" *American Philosophical Quarterly* 36/2: 115–30.

Howard-Snyder, Daniel and Paul Moser, eds. 2001. *Divine Hiddenness: New Essays*. New York: Cambridge University Press.

Howard-Snyder, Daniel and John O'Leary-Hawthorne. 1998. "Transworld Sanctity and Plantinga's Free Will Defense." *International Journal for Philosophy of Religion* 44: 1–21.

Howard-Snyder, Daniel, Michael Bergmann, and William Rowe. 2001. "An Exchange on the Problem of Evil." In *God and the Problem of Evil*, ed. William Rowe, 124–58. Malden, MA: Blackwell.

Hume, David. 1947. *Dialogues Concerning Natural Religion*. Ed. Norman Kemp Smith. New York: Thomas Nelson & Sons.

Kvanvig, Jonathan. 2001. "Divine Hiddenness: What Is the Problem?" In *Divine Hiddenness: New Essays*, ed. Daniel Howard-Snyder and Paul Moser, 149–63. New York: Cambridge University Press.

Mackie, J. L. 1955. "Evil and Omnipotence." *Mind* 64: 200–212.

Mackie, J. L. 1990. "Evil and Omnipotence." In *The Problem of Evil*, ed. Marilyn McCord Adams and Robert Merrihew Adams, 25–37. New York: Oxford University Press.

McBrayer, Justin and Daniel Howard-Snyder, eds. 2013. *The Blackwell Companion to the Problem of Evil*. Chichester: Wiley-Blackwell.

McBrayer, Justin and Philip Swenson. 2012. "Scepticism About the Argument from Divine Hiddenness." *Religious Studies* 48: 129–50.

McBrayer, Justin. Forthcoming. "Sceptical Theism." In *The Routledge Encyclopedia of Philosophy*. http://www.rep.routledge.com/about [accessed 04/03/2014].

McCloskey, H. J. 1960. "God and Evil." *Philosophical Quarterly* 10: 97–114.

Murray, Michael. 1993. "Coercion and the Hiddenness of God." *American Philosophical Quarterly* 30/1: 27–38.

Murray, Michael. 2001. "Deus Absconditus." In *Divine Hiddenness: New Essays*, ed. Daniel Howard-Snyder and Paul Moser, 62–82. New York: Cambridge University Press.

Murray, Michael. 2011. *Nature Red in Tooth and Claw: Theism and the Problem of Animal Suffering*. Oxford: Oxford University Press.

Nagel, Thomas. 1997. *The Last Word*. New York: Oxford University Press.

Nelkin, Dana. 2012. *Making Sense of Freedom and Responsibility*. New York: Oxford University Press.

O'Connor, Timothy. 2009. "Theodicies and Human Nature: Dostoevsky on the Saint as Witness." In *Metaphysics and God: Essays in Honor of Eleonore Stump*, ed. Kevin Timpe, 175–87. New York: Routledge.

Oppy, Graham. 2011. "Ontological Arguments." In *The Stanford Encyclopedia of Philosophy* (Spring 2013 Edition), ed. Edward N. Zalta. http://plato.stanford.edu/entries/ontological-arguments/ [accessed 04/03/2014].

Pascal, Blaise. 1995. *Pensées and Other Writings*. Trans. Honor Levi. New York: Oxford University Press.

Pereboom, Derk. 2001. *Living Without Free Will*. Cambridge: Cambridge University Press.

Perszyk, Ken. 1998. "Free Will Defense With and Without Molinism." *International Journal for Philosophy of Religion* 44/3: 29–64.

Perszyk, Ken, ed. 2011. *Molinism: The Contemporary Debate*. New York: Oxford University Press.

Pinnock, Clark, Richard Rice, John Sanders, William Hasker, and David Basinger. 1994. *The Openness of God: A Biblical Challenge to the Traditional Understanding of God*. Downers Grove, IL: InterVarsity Press.

Plantinga, Alvin. 1967. *God and Other Minds: A Study of the Rational Justification of Belief in God*. Ithaca, NY: Cornell University Press. Reprinted in Plantinga 1990; page numbers refer to this latter edition.

Plantinga, Alvin. 1974. *God, Freedom, and Evil*. Grand Rapids, MI: Eerdmans.

Plantinga, Alvin. 1988. "Positive Epistemic Status and Proper Function." *Philosophical Perspectives* 2: 1–50.

Plantinga, Alvin. 1990. "God, Evil, and the Metaphysics of Freedom." In *The Problem of Evil*, ed. Marilyn McCord Adams and Robert Merrihew Adams, 83–109. New York: Oxford.

Plantinga, Alvin. 2000. *Warranted Christian Belief*. New York: Oxford University Press.

Plantinga, Alvin. 2004. "Supralapsarianism, or 'O Felix Culpa'." In *Christian Faith and the Problem of Evil*, ed. Peter van Inwagen. Grand Rapids, MI: Wm. B. Eerdmans Publishing Co.

Plantinga, Alvin. 2009. "Transworld Depravity, Transworld Sanctity, and Uncooperative Essences." *Philosophy and Phenomenological Research* 78: 165–77.

Poston, Ted. 2014. "Social Evil." In *Oxford Studies in Philosophy of Religion*, ed. Jonathan Kvanvig. Oxford: Oxford University Press.

Poston, Ted and Trent Dougherty. 2007. "Divine Hiddenness and the Nature of Belief." *Religious Studies* 43/2: 183–98.

Pruss, Alexander. 2012. "A Counterexample to Plantinga's Free Will Defense." *Faith and Philosophy* 29: 400–15.

Rea, Michael. 2013. "Skeptical Theism and the 'Too Much Skepticism' Objection." In *The Blackwell Companion to the Problem of Evil*, ed. Justin McBrayer and Daniel Howard-Snyder, 482–506. Chichester: Wiley-Blackwell.

Rhoda, Alan. 2008. "Generic Open Theism and Some Varieties Thereof." *Religious Studies* 44: 225–34.

Rowe, William. 1979. "The Problem of Evil and Some Varieties of Atheism." *American Philosophical Quarterly* 16/4: 335–41. Reprinted in Howard-Snyder 1996; page numbers refer to this latter edition.

Rowe, William. 1996. "The Evidential Argument from Evil: A Second Look." In *The Evidential Argument from Evil*, ed. Daniel Howard-Snyder, 262–85. Bloomington, IN: Indiana University Press.

Rowe, William, ed. 2001. *God and the Problem of Evil*. Malden, MA: Blackwell.

Russell, Bruce. 1996. "Defenseless." In *The Evidential Argument from Evil*, ed. Daniel Howard-Snyder, 193–205. Bloomington, IN: Indiana University Press.

Schellenberg, J. L. 1993. *Divine Hiddenness and Human Reason*. Ithaca, NY: Cornell University Press.

Schellenberg, J. L. 2005a. "The Hiddenness Argument Revisited (I)." *Religious Studies* 41/2: 201–15.

Schellenberg, J. L. 2005b. "The Hiddenness Argument Revisited (II)." *Religious Studies* 41/3: 287–303.

Speak, Daniel. 2013. "Free Will and Soul-Making Theodicies." In *The Blackwell Companion to the Problem of Evil*, ed. Justin McBrayer and Daniel Howard-Snyder, 205–20. Chichester: Wiley-Blackwell.

Stump, Eleonore. 1985. "The Problem of Evil." *Faith and Philosophy* 2/4: 392–423.

Stump, Eleonore. 1986. "Dante's Hell, Aquinas's Moral Theory, and the Love of God." *Canadian Journal of Philosophy* 16/2: 181–96.

Stump, Eleonore, ed. 1993. *Reasoned Faith*. Ithaca, NY: Cornell University Press.

Stump, Eleonore. 2012. *Wandering In Darkness: Narrative and the Problem of Suffering*. New York: Oxford University Press.

Swinburne, Richard. 1998. *Providence and the Problem of Evil*. New York: Oxford University Press.

Swinburne, Richard. 2004. *The Existence of God*. New York: Oxford University Press.

Swinburne, Richard. 2013. *Mind, Brain, and Free Will*. New York: Oxford University Press.

Tomberlin, James and Peter van Inwagen, eds. 1985. *Alvin Plantinga*. Dordrecht: Reidel Publishing.

Tooley, Michael. 2012. "The Problem of Evil." In *The Stanford Encyclopedia of Philosophy* (Spring 2013 Edition), ed. Edward N. Zalta. http://plato.stanford.edu/entries/evil/ [accessed 04/03/2014].

Trakakis, Nick. 2005. "The Evidential Problem of Evil." In *The Internet Encyclopedia of Philosophy*, ed. James Fieser and Bradley Dowden. http://www.iep.utm.edu/evil-evi/ [accessed 04/03/2014].

Trakakis, Nick. 2007. *The God Beyond Belief: In Defence of William Rowe's Evidential Argument from Evil*. Dordrecht: Springer Verlag.

Trakakis, Nick. Forthcoming. "Anti-theodicy." In *The Cambridge Companion to the Problem of Evil*, ed. Chad Mesiter and Paul K. Moser. Cambridge: Cambridge University Press.

van Inwagen, Peter. 1988. "The Magnitude, Duration, and Distribution of Evil: A Theodicy." *Philosophical Topics* 16: 161–87.

van Inwagen, Peter. 1991. "The Problem of Evil, the Problem of Air, and the Problem of Silence." *Philosophical Perspectives* 5: 135–65.

van Inwagen, Peter. 2001. "What Is the Problem of the Hiddenness of God?" In *Divine Hiddenness: New Essays*, ed. Daniel Howard-Snyder and Paul Moser, 24–32. New York: Cambridge University Press.

van Inwagen, Peter. 2006. *The Problem of Evil*. New York: Oxford University Press.

Wainwright, William. 2001. "Jonathan Edwards and the Hiddenness of God." In *Divine Hiddenness: New Essays*, ed. Daniel Howard-Snyder and Paul Moser, 98–119. New York: Cambridge University Press.

Watson, Gary. 2004. *Agency and Answerability*. New York: Oxford University Press.

Wilks, Ian. 2009. "Skeptical Theism and Empirical Unfalsifiability." *Faith and Philosophy* 26/1: 64–76.

Wykstra, Stephen. 1996. "Rowe's Noseeum Arguments from Evil." In *The Evidential Argument from Evil*, ed. Daniel Howard-Snyder, 126–50. Bloomington, IN: Indiana University Press.

Index

actualization 34–5, 37–8
Adams, Marilyn 106, 119,
120, 123, 125, 126, 131
Adams, Robert 25, 119
Aiken, Henry 130
Alighieri, Dante 107
Almeida, Michael 66, 68
Alston, William 39, 56, 133
animal suffering 50, 54, 122
annihilationism 106
anthropomorphism 108–9
Aquinas, Thomas 23, 107, 126
atheism 6, 11, 116–18
St. Augustine 3

Bergmann, Michael 56, 135,
138
The Brothers Karamazov 11,
12, 14, 115, 127–8, 129
Byrne, Peter 64

Capes, Justin 132
Christology 125, 139
Clarke, Randolph 41–3, 132,
138
common theism
see theism
consequentialism 108

defeaters of belief 65, 112
defense 7, 8, 10, 90–3, 95
Dennett, Daniel 99
DeRose, Keith 44, 131
Descartes, René 131
*Dialogues Concerning Natural
Religion* 19
divine hiddenness 6, 9, 71–93
Dostoevsky, Fyodor 11–14,
115–16, 127–8, 129
Dougherty, Trent 138
Draper, Paul 135–6, 137
*The Dream of the Ridiculous
Man* 12–14, 115–16, 128

Epicurus 3, 22
epistemic humility 57, 58
epistemic unreasonableness
of believing in God 48–9
eschatology 104–7
Evidential argument from
evil 6, 9, 47–72
Evil 5, 6
kinds of evil 37
sources of evil 14

Fischer, John Martin 132
Flew, Antony 40, 130

Flint, Thomas 132
Frances, Bryan 133
free will 30–8, 54, 61, 81–2,
    97–9, 100–1, 104, 107,
    132, 135
  compatibilism 40–3, 97–9,
    132
  libertarianism/
    incompatibilism 34,
    39–43, 97–9, 100–1, 104,
    132
Free Will Defense 25–39, 40,
    45–6, 97–8, 119, 122

Gale, Richard 66
God
  God as perfectly
    loving 76–8, 86–7
  constraints on God 23, 24,
    31, 34, 35, 46, 61, 107,
    133
  human relationship with
    God 9, 76–8, 83, 86–7,
    97, 105–6
  omnibenevolence of God 5,
    22, 53, 57–9, 64, 107, 120
  omnipotence of God 4, 22,
    34
  omniscience of God 4, 53,
    57–61, 133
good parent analogy
  see parent analogy
goodness proposition 22, 28,
    29
gratuitous evils 51–3, 59–61,
    63, 108

Hardin, Garrett 122
Hasker, William 133
Hawthorne, John 44, 45, 46,
    131, 132
hell 106–7
Hick, John 99–102, 105–6,
    138–9

horrendous evils 119–20
Howard-Snyder, Daniel 44, 45,
    46, 91, 123, 131, 132,
    135, 137, 139
Hume, David 2, 3, 19, 130,
    135
hypothesis of indifference
    135–6

impossibility claim 96, 97
inculpable unbelief
    see reasonable unbelief

Kvanvig, Jonathan 75

Leibniz, Gottfried 19, 94–5
Leibniz' Lapse 34–5, 46
Lisbon earthquake 94–5
logical argument from evil 6,
    9, 19–46
logical contradiction 21–4
  of the theistic set 21, 22,
    26–7

McBrayer, Justin 92, 123, 137,
    138, 139
McCloskey, H.J. 130
Mackie, J.L. 19, 20–36, 40–1,
    45–6, 78, 130, 131
massively irregular
    world 103–4
middle knowledge 131, 133,
    137
Milton, John 117
miracles 103
Molinism 131, 132–3, 137
Moore, G.E. 62, 63
Moorean Shift 62–6, 111
Moser, Paul 137
Murray, Michael 80, 82,
    122–3, 137

Nagel, Thomas 136
natural evil 37, 38, 122

necessary truths 27, 33
Nelkin, Dana 132
noetic effects of sin 80
nonhuman agents 38
"noseeum" inference 56–8, 67,
    85–6

O'Connor, Timothy 129
Open Theism 61, 62, 133,
    134, 135
Oppy, Graham 64, 66, 68

parent analogy 71, 88, 89
Pascal, Blaise 74, 137
St. Paul 79, 82, 137
Pereboom, Derk 41, 42, 43, 99
Perszyk, Ken 132, 133
Pinnock, Clark 134
Plantinga, Alvin 9, 25–40,
    43–6, 56, 64, 80, 97,
    109–10, 119, 130, 131,
    132–3, 134, 139
possibility of evil 31–3
possible worlds 26, 33–4
Poston, Ted 121–2, 138
power proposition 22
Principle of Credulity 110
problem of evil
    history of the problem of
        evil 3
    philosophical versus personal
        problems of evil 16
    problem of evil and
        Christianity 123–6, 139
    problem of evil and non-
        Christian religions 123–4,
        126
    problem of evil and
        empathy 16–18
    problem of evil for
        atheism 116–18
problem of goodness 116–17
problem of profound evil 10,
    118
Pruss, Alexander 132

Ravizza, Mark 132
Rea, Michael 135
reasonable unbelief 74, 77–81,
    83, 84
reasons
    having reasons versus
        existence of reasons
        69–70
    reasons for permitting
        evil 60, 67–70, 112, 134
Rhoda, Alan 134
Rowe, William 39, 40, 49–58,
    60, 62–5, 70–2, 91, 111,
    133, 134, 135, 136, 138
Russell, Bruce 66, 68

Schellenberg, J.L. 75, 76–89,
    91, 136–7, 138
skeptical theism 9, 56, 66–8,
    84–6, 88–93, 136, 138
social evil 121–2
soul-building
    see soul-making
soul-making 54, 99–102, 104,
    138
stable natural laws 102–4
Stump, Eleonore 106–7,
    125–6
suffering 89–90, 100–2, 126
Swenson, Philip 137, 138
Swinburne, Richard 82, 102,
    106, 110–12, 113, 123,
    124–5, 138, 139

theism 4, 10
    definition of theism 4
    rationality or irrationality of
        theism 3, 10, 21, 27,
        110–12
    theism in Christianity 4
theistic set 4, 25, 26, 27, 30
theodicy 8, 9, 10, 93, 94–114,
    138
Tomberlin, James 110
Tooley, Michael 64

Trakakis, Nick 64, 107, 133, 135
transworld depravity 36, 43, 44, 46, 132

universalism 105

value claim 96, 97
value of being of use 123

van Inwagen, Peter 56, 75, 102, 103, 104, 110, 113, 135, 136, 139
Voltaire 94

Wainwright, William 80
Watson, Gary 132
Wilks, Ian 66
Wykstra, Stephen 56, 134